How to Win A...

CW00421239

124

VIEW

ROBERT ALLEN

How to Win Arguments

THE COMPLETE GUIDE TO COMING OUT ON TOP

Thorsons
An Imprint of HarperCollins*Publishers*

Thorsons
An Imprint of HarperCollins*Publishers*
77–85 Fulham Palace Road,
Hammersmith, London W6 8JB
1160 Battery Street,
San Francisco, California 94111–1213

Published by Thorsons 1996
1   3   5   7   9   10   8   6   4   2

A catalogue record for this book is
available from the British Library

ISBN 0 7225 3159 1

Typeset by Harper Phototypesetters Limited
Northampton, England
Printed in Great Britain by
HarperCollinsManufacturing Glasgow

Contents

Heated Exchanges

How good are you at getting your own way? Do you usually persuade people to do what you want or do you sometimes feel that you get put upon by others who have greater powers of persuasion? The subject is, of course, a delicate one. In theory 'getting your own way' is rather frowned upon and our parents and teachers always discouraged us from being too pushy. However, there will always be ruthlessly ambitious people who have no qualms about pushing others around to get what they want out of life. Unless we live a life of total seclusion, we are bound to come up against such people, and must be prepared to deal with them if we don't want to be pushed around ourselves. We may try to live a quiet life away from the fighting, but those of us with goals and ambitions are unlikely to achieve them without stepping into the ring. The rules of the playground, though uncivilized, dominate our lives to the grave.

As humans we live, work and play together in social groups such as families, firms, institutions and nations, all in social cooperation with each other. However, we are, each of us, autonomous: we have free will. And like other animals, even social animals, we are competitive. How does the autonomous individual seek to influence the behaviour of the social group? By argument. We seek to persuade others to our point of view.

However, as we all know, that is a bland description of a process that is, in practice, decidedly colourful. For human nature dictates that the process of persuasion is invested with such importance that when we are thwarted the result might be anything from mild frustration to anger, violence or even, in extreme cases, outright war. This makes argument, and how we can get our own way, a subject of compelling interest to us all.

The truth, unattractive as it may be, is that we all argue constantly. Much of this argument occurs at a fairly innocuous level and we therefore tend not to notice what we are doing. In any case, because we have been cautioned from our earliest years that loud, public disagreement is in bad taste, we often try to pretend it is not happening. We say things like, 'We weren't arguing; we were just discussing.' If we come across people involved in an unseemly squabble (and we are conditioned to regard any quarrel not involving ourselves as unseemly), our usual reaction is to turn away. 'I wasn't going to get involved in an argument,' we tell our friends later. The result is that argument, like death, is a subject we tend to avoid thinking about. This is a pity. For if the objective of argument is to persuade, then what we are doing is to make ourselves less effective persuaders. Also, as we shall see later, the process of argument is a uniquely human way of providing a safety valve for powerful feelings. Many animals indulge in threat displays that resolve conflict without risking damage to the participants, but humans who feel frustrated by the lack of cooperation shown by others can engage in a whole series of verbal manoeuvres before they resort to beating each other over the head with a brick. In societies where this safety valve is deliberately blocked, violence may be explosive and unpredictable.

So let's cast aside our natural reluctance and take a good,

hard look at how we argue. By studying the processes involved we may be able to learn to make ourselves more effective at using them. Perhaps we should take as our model the self-defence class. It is one of the basic principles of self-defence that, because you will not have time to think when you are actually attacked, you should prepare yourself in advance to the point where your reactions are fluent and automatic. Argument is often bound up with human aggression and with consequently heightened levels of emotion. It follows that we should practise before any dire necessity arises.

Arguments are never the verbal free-for-all we might assume. They are highly structured and there are many distinct categories, all with their own rules and tactics. It is possible to identify a number of elements in all arguments, including emotional content, concern for the truth, status of the partici-pants and self-interest of the participants. However, the rela-tive proportions of such elements in different types of argument can be a very important guide to the tactics that we should adopt in a given situation. This process of analysing arguments and learning in advance how to respond forms a large part of this book. We must understand that a tiff with our partner is different in both kind and scale from, say, a legal wrangle conducted in the courts. Both are arguments and will be carried on according to rules, but they will be as different from each other as Rugby Union and Rugby League. (As my former games master succinctly put it, 'Same shaped ball, different games.')

We shall look at tactics used in argument and learn how to make them work effectively for us. There is a whole section devoted to different tactics, both aggressive and defensive, that will help you argue better. They have been culled from witnessing many hours of actual argument and are recommended for their efficacy. We shall also look at the 'dirty tricks' of argument and see what can be done to guard against them. This brings me to an important point. Much of what goes on in argument is the sort of behaviour we are not proud of. It shows us at our worst and not as we would wish to see ourselves. When we argue, we may have all sorts of justifications for what we are doing, but the plain truth is that we are trying to get our own way. Quite often we do so directly at the expense of someone else and in the full knowledge that our victory may inflict damage on our opponent. I am merely commenting on how these ends are achieved. I am not recommending that you should suddenly adopt a repertoire of dodgy tactics and use them to bully and cajole those around you to do your will. Moral decisions about what is fair and what is not are left, at all times, up to you.

We are also going to consider what 'winning' and 'losing' really mean. It is interesting that we so often regard argument as a competition. In spite of all those earnest American scholars of Management Studies, with their talk of 'principled negotiation', most of the time we want to see a winner and a loser. But is it enough merely to outwit your opponent in a battle of verbal skill or do you require some specific result that will be to your advantage? The two aims are often incompatible. Also we have to bear in mind those oriental mystics who would sagely point out to us that, in many cases, losing (or appearing to lose) is winning. Actually this insight is not confined to Zen monks and Taoist sages – they share it with most women, especially the married ones.

This brings us to another point. Do men and women argue differently? Do they employ different tactics, argue about different things or have different concepts of what constitutes winning and losing? Are women happier than men to reach a consensus? These are some of the issues to which we shall be paying attention.

Also we shall look at the psychology of argument and, using techniques from a number of different disciplines, try to understand the mechanics at work when we argue. We shall devise strategies for a more effective use of arguing skills and try to use psychological insights to understand an opponent's motives and strategy. In particular, the techniques of transactional analysis will be recommended as a means of understanding some of the forces at work in an argument.

I must also add a personal comment about self-help books. They have always bothered me. Surely the reader is entitled to ask, 'Who is this person and what gives him the right to lecture me?' It is a fair question and is seldom answered. You are expected to take the author on trust. My answer is this: I assume that since you are reading this book you feel that your arguing skills could do with improvement. Naturally bossy, assertive people are unlikely to have strayed further than the front cover. I am not a professional in the field of argument (though I do have some psychological training). I have made a study of argument because the subject fascinates me. Like most people I have often felt that I could have given a better account of myself in arguments and have regretted lost opportunities. However, the sort of writer who happily advises shy people to smile and offer a new acquaintance a friendly handshake is rather missing the point. If they were capable of doing that they would not be shy in the first place. So all the advice I intend to give is intensely practical and has been thoroughly researched and tested. If an idea has proved reliable I shall recommend it warmly, but where a particular tactic is of only marginal value I shall mention it with an appropriate 'health warning' attached. I am certain that you will not finish the book without having learned a number of skills that will improve your arguing ability significantly.

Although you will find a list of recommended books in the appendix these will not help you half as much as observing arguments for yourself. There is no problem about this, they are happening around us all the time. Any bus queue, crowded shopping centre, car park, railway station, TV debate, radio phone-in or playground squabble will provide you with ample opportunity to study. The art is to listen attentively and take a dispassionate interest in what is going on. This is a difficult habit for many of us to cultivate because we have such a deeply ingrained dislike of hearing people bicker. We know full well that we are only a hair's breadth away from violence and our instinct is to put as much distance between ourselves and the cause of the trouble as possible. But try not to run away. Most arguments are merely ludicrous rather than threatening. Most of the anger is bluff and will never lead to blows. If you watch what is happening closely you will see that much of what is happening is ritualized and predictable. Once you understand the ritual you are well placed to control its direction. The techniques that are being used effectively by one arguer can be easily adapted for use by yourself. And because so few people bother to study argument properly you, who have taken the time to do so, will be in a position to win.

One final point. Throughout the book, in the interests of brevity, I have used the male third person singular pronouns. No sinister sexist sub-text should be found in this; unless otherwise stated, my remarks apply as much to women as to men.

CHAPTER ONE

Things You Should Know

What Makes an Argument?

The question seems unnecessary. After all, argument is a universal human activity in which we all engage as regularly and naturally as breathing. Even if we have never given much thought to the theory behind it, we have enough practical experience to recognize an argument the moment we become embroiled in one or hear others engaged in verbal conflict.

However, if we are to avoid misunderstandings later there are a few points to sort out at the start. *Chambers Twentieth Century Dictionary* says that to argue is 'to discuss with reasoning'. Reasoning? Two cars collide on a cold, wet Monday morning in the rush hour. One, driven by a 25-year-old junior executive, a sporty job with a souped-up engine and go-faster stripes down the sides, was going much too fast and skidded in the wet. The other is driven by a woman doing the school run with two small children in the back seat. How much reasoning would you expect to hear? Would a calm, impartial and mutually satisfactory discussion be the most likely outcome? Experience tells us that the ensuing argument would probably be high on emotion, low on reasoning.

Eventually the police appear and tempers are calmed. But

while the adults talk, one of the children steals the other's teddy bear and throws it into the front seat. Will they sort out their differences by an exchange of reasons? Even the most limited observation of young children will make you aware that reason rarely plays a part in such exchanges. People are not wholly rational creatures and their arguments are seldom based purely on reason. Of course, human beings know how to use reason and may well do so when trying to justify their actions but that is a far cry from acting consistently in a rational manner. Most human arguments are conducted in an atmosphere that reeks of emotion, manipulation, self-interest, false reasoning, bigotry and propaganda. This book aims to show you how to survive that jungle.

In America there is currently a great vogue for analysing and teaching negotiation skills. The business section of every bookshop and library has handbooks offering to improve the reader's negotiating technique. University courses are offered to those hoping that their business careers will be enhanced by a talent for negotiating. Harvard boasts the distinguished Harvard Negotiation Project whose aim is to 'develop and disseminate improved methods of negotiation and mediation'. This morning's newspaper even contains an advertisement for a twenty-page report which for £19.70 promises to reveal '38 of the dirtiest tactics used by professional negotiators' and '. . . how to handle them'.

However, although negotiation is one part of the area we shall be discussing, it is by no means the whole of it. There is a fundamental difference between negotiation and argument.

In a negotiation, both sides, however much they try to look detached and disinterested, are searching for an agreement. Naturally they want the most advantageous settlement they can get and during the course of the discussions they will try all manner of stratagems to achieve that aim. If they feel that there is no possibility of getting a sufficiently favourable settlement then the negotiations may be broken off for some time, but still deep down they want agreement. They may even need one desperately. Take a look, for example, at the war that has followed the break-up of the former Yugoslavia. Much of the time peace seems impossible and repeatedly the various factions have met to negotiate and have then parted without reaching a settlement. Yet all the parties are well aware that no state can exist in a condition of permanent civil war and therefore, at some stage, a negotiated settlement will have to be found. Similar situations exist in the Middle East, Northern Ireland, Rwanda and many other world trouble spots. However bitter the differences that divide one side from another, there is always a need for people who live in close proximity to get on with each other. Since human society is impossible without that element of cooperation, in the end negotiation must always be the answer. Even the Troubles in Northern Ireland, which have persisted for twenty-five years and are based upon disagreements hundreds of years old are at last being settled by negotiation.

Argument is fundamentally different. In an argument the parties may not want a settlement at all, ever. For example, where two rival politicians are debating a point on television it is a forgone conclusion that neither will change his or her position or make any concession at all to the other. That was never the point of the argument. The aim of each contestant is to convert as many voters as possible to his or her own point of view. Similarly, there are many cases where the only point of an argument is to chasten and humiliate an opponent by scoring a victory in a battle of verbal skill. The substance of the argument is purely secondary to the emotional battle that forms the subtext. Take as an example a couple about to divorce who are trying to decide who gets custody of the children. We have all heard of cases where concern for the children's welfare is outweighed by a desire to score an emotional and legal victory over a former spouse who has become a hated opponent. Couples have been known to inflict enormous mental and emotional damage on themselves and their children in such a struggle.

Negotiation experts who offer advice like 'separate the people from the problem', or 'deal rationally with irrational people' are missing the point. Frequently people enjoy being irrational. There are many areas of human life where arguments exist for their own sake and are tied up with issues of power and status, not to mention sheer bloody-mindedness.

The American psychologist Eric Berne described arguments as a clash between the images we all carry in our minds. He explained that none of us has an objective view of reality but instead we perceive things through the filter of our own personality. With time these perceived images become fixed and we are increasingly loath to change them. Berne cited the instance of an able-bodied man who loses a leg. It may take some considerable time for him to alter his image of himself from that of a fit person to that of a handicapped one. He may continue to 'feel' the leg even though it is no longer there and, even when he seems to have accepted his altered condition there may be times when he dreams of himself as once again being able-bodied.

The problem comes when we are forced to abandon an image to which we still wish to cling. Sam had admired Katie for about six months before he got up the courage to ask her out. He was not especially good-looking or well off and she was remarkably pretty and vivacious. To his surprise she accepted. The date was a great success, they found they had a lot in common and before long they were going steady. However, Sam's best friend Joe was unhappy with the situation. Once he and Sam had spent much of their leisure time hanging around together. Now Sam was usually too occupied with Katie to devote much time to his old friend. Joe heard gossip that Katie was well known for amusing herself with someone for a while and then dumping him in favour of a new conquest. Eventually Joe spotted Katie with another man and felt he had to warn Sam that his girlfriend was unfaithful. Sam was in no mood to hear Katie slandered. In his eyes she was just about the best thing that had ever happened to him and it was not hard to guess that Joe's motive was simply jealousy. An argument developed, became quite heated and soon the two friends split up and ceased to speak to each other.

Who was right? We don't know. From our point of view it doesn't really matter. Probably there was some truth in the accusation that Joe was jealous but, all the same, he may have genuinely thought that he had a duty to save his friend from what he saw as the clutches of a devious woman. That is the point about arguments. The 'real' facts are often extremely hard to discover. What is much more important is how people feel about the facts. Sam felt strongly attracted to Katie. Most people are lucky enough to have had the experience of liking someone so much that they can't bear to hear him criticized. Joe was trying to let what he saw as the cold light of reality break into his friend's romantic dream. It was the fundamental incompatibility of the two men's images of Katie that caused the row.

If we think about this tale a little further another interesting point emerges. Surely the strength of a particular image must have a bearing on the situation. If Sam's faith in Katie had been completely rock solid he would have been able to dismiss Joe's advice with a pitying smile. He might not even have felt much offended. Imagine, for example, that someone accused your mother of being a spy for a foreign power. The idea would seem so ludicrous that your first reaction would be to laugh it off. Your confidence in her innocence would be so strong that it would take tremendous pressure to crack it. So we can see that one of the first lessons to be learned in argument is confidence in your own cause. As long as you are firmly convinced that your image is the one that best describes reality you will be very hard to budge even when, to all other eyes, you are in the wrong.

Richard, a scientist friend of mine, is a convinced and passionate Christian. He is also a brilliant speaker with a tremendous natural gift for oratory. I once organized a conference about the developments we could expect to see in the next millennium. To add some excitement to the proceedings I asked Richard to debate the notion that in the coming century Christianity would die. As a matter of interest we asked for a vote at the beginning of the debate to establish the beliefs of the audience and found that we had about forty atheists, fifteen Christians and twenty agnostics.

In the debate Jim, another scientist, put the case for the death of Christianity with great panache. He was a witty, practised speaker and completely familiar with all the pros and cons of this argument (it was a personal favourite of his and he had gone over it with many opponents in the past). Then Richard spoke. Intellectually his speech was not a patch on Jim's and, to a non-believer, it sounded far too personal and emotional, but he had one great advantage. Richard felt he knew God personally. He spoke with such utter rock-solid conviction that, by the end of the debate, the subject of which had by now changed from the death of Christianity to the existence of God, something interesting had happened. A final vote about religious beliefs showed that, as you might expect, none of the atheists and Christians had changed their view. However, among the agnostics Richard's speech had convinced about ten to change their mind, while Jim had persuaded none. Thus, although Jim won the debate on a show of hands, the true lesson for me was that a powerful belief in what you are saying is one of the biggest assets you can have in an argument.

Elements of an Argument

Arguments can seem like a verbal free-for-all in which the participants simply hurl at each other whatever missiles come to hand. However, there are a number of elements that always contribute to the making of any argument and the way in which these elements combine will tell you much about the form the argument may be expected to take. What are these elements? Here's a list.

Concern for Truth

It is always worth considering to what extent the parties are trying to reach the truth. Of course, your opponent's 'truth' may not be yours but, if you feel that he is trying, by his own lights, to get at a rational analysis of the situation then you will have more confidence in his arguments and be willing to give them a more sympathetic hearing. If, on the other hand, you are pretty sure that your opponent is only concerned to get his own way, to score a victory for the body he represents, or to inflict a humiliating defeat on you, then you will be suspicious of any arguments he may use.

Unfortunately, concern for truth is usually one of the rarest elements in any argument. Even among scientists and academics who spend their whole lives trying to deepen their understanding of their chosen field, it is common to find a degree of partisanship that does not do the truth any favours at all. Evidence that supports their own view is put forward while contrary findings are belittled or ignored.

The stories of this happening are too many to tell here but, as just one illustration, let's take the example of the Wright brothers and their experiments with a heavier-than-air flying machine. Although their efforts were widely reported, the experts persisted in dismissing them as poppycock. Heavier-than-air flight was impossible and so it followed that what these two charlatans were doing must be a fraud. The early tests took place in a field that lay beside a railroad track and were witnessed by many rail passengers as they passed by, but that counted for nothing in the eyes of the experts. You will quickly realize that if you get involved in an argument where a genuine quest for the truth is involved you will be extremely fortunate. When both parties struggle to reach a deeper level of truth by engaging in constructive argument they are experiencing one of the mental processes that sets us apart from our fellow primates. We rightly regard this phenomenon with great respect. So much so that we do not normally refer to it as 'argument' at all, but as discussion.

Self-interest

Another important element to be aware of is the extent to which the participants in an argument stand to gain from the outcome. The most obvious example is where there is some material gain in money or goods that is eagerly sought by the parties. There is also the question of a gain in status that comes from winning an argument but this is such an important element in arguments that it deserves, and will get, a section all to itself.

When getting involved in an argument it is as well to consider just what is at stake financially. Ask yourself what, if anything, your opponent stands to gain. This will give you great insight into the lengths to which he may go to defeat you. An argument over whose turn it is to buy the next round in the pub is likely to be fought less tenaciously than one over the ownership of, say, a champion racehorse or a valuable building site. This should not be taken as an infallible guide (see the sections on Status and Emotional Content), but it must be urgently considered.

There is another important consideration. People involved in arguments may not always tell the truth. They may either lie deliberately to deceive you about their true motives or they may even mislead themselves about what those motives are. It can be very hard indeed to unmask a good liar. The idea that liars look shifty or give themselves away with special body-language signs is laughably naive. When you are confused about who is telling the truth it is as well to consider what each participant has to gain. This may not be an infallible guide but it is often the only clue you will get.

What of your own motives? It is in the nature of argument

that sometimes you will merely be trying to get your own way. Truth, Justice or the Greater Good will simply not enter your thoughts. This is human nature. However, if you are aware that that is what you are doing then you will be in a much better position to handle the argument. Naturally you will rationalize your position so that you feel justified in getting your own way (this is a psychological trick we all use as a matter of course). But if you can retain some vestige of impartiality you will be able to construct an argument that at least appears to be based on a desire to get at a just solution.

You should also weigh your advantage very carefully against the possible costs of getting what you want. For example, if you do battle with A over this matter and win you may feel very pleased with yourself. On the other hand, suppose your relationship with A is ongoing and you know that soon you will have to argue over matters that are even more important to you. What do you do? Perhaps by giving him a fair deal this time you will soften him up for a hard argument when it really matters. On the other hand you may reason that if you thrash the pants off A right now you will be able to use your psychological advantage to overcome him again in the future. Your actions in this situation will depend mainly on your reading of A's character, but an accurate assessment of the material gains to be made will tell just how far it is worth going with your argument. Would you, for example, be wise to offend someone mortally over a matter that was only worth a few pounds? Arguments quickly get out of hand, tempers become inflamed, pride suffers and before you know where you are you may find yourself engaged in a major war over something that is worth only a trifle.

Status

Anyone who has read this far will be in no doubt that I do not have much faith in human beings as rational creatures. A glance at today's news headlines (any day, any country) will bear me out. That is why the issue of status assumes such importance in the realm of argument. It is utterly irrational, a throwback to our animal ancestors, and yet it still exerts an iron control over our behaviour. One can readily understand why baboons may depend for their success on organising their family groups on the basis of status. But people? The thinking apes? Unfortunately it is all too true.

Status in arguments is seen best within a business environment or in some highly structured organization such as the army or police. Anyone who has ever worked in an office or factory will have seen a boss who is always right, no matter how wrong he may be. Bosses like this don't argue about the facts of a case (they may well be ignorant of them and, in any case, they regard them as largely irrelevant). No, their chief concern will be that by pursuing a particular course successfully (getting their own way), and putting down any opposition they may encounter, they get to stay Chief Baboon.

Subordinates will often play along with this game by deliberately deferring to the boss and letting his opinions hold sway even when they know he is wrong. In that way they help to confirm his status and thus bolster their own position in the pecking order. One of the features of a pecking order is that people do not mind it as long as it remains unchanged. In fact they will engage in regular rituals that are designed specifically to reconfirm the order. However, someone who dares to try to upset the status quo will spark off the bitterest of status arguments.

Another interesting feature of status is that the people who concern themselves with it do not have to be 'important'. It is not only officers and gentlemen who worry about their pecking orders. Think for a moment of the stock comedy figures of the mild-mannered gentlefolk who organize the church flower rota. Anyone who has experienced the intrigues and political chicanery attendant upon a church flower rota will know that the issue of status is just as important to the meek and humble as to the high and mighty.

Emotion

Arguments are frequently very emotional occasions. It is surprising that, even when we think we are engaged in a rational discussion about some matter of objective fact, a contrary opinion can stir feelings of resentment or even anger. The truth is that no one likes to be contradicted or, even worse, proved wrong. Issues of status are immediately brought into play in almost any argument. You may not care two hoots about a particular topic until someone tells you that your opinion on the subject is wrong. Then you may well feel inclined to fight to the death to prove yourself right.

This is a human reaction and, as such, we have to live with it. There is no point trying to pretend that you are some sort of superhuman being who is not affected by the heady emotions attached to an argument. However, if you are aware of the extent to which you may be emotionally involved in what is being said you may be able to stand aside from yourself just enough to prevent falling into the worst excesses.

It used to be said that the forbidden topics of polite conversation were sex, politics and religion. Nowadays many people pride themselves on getting to grips with the issues of the day and having full and frank discussions on things that really matter. There are far fewer taboos about what can be discussed. However, there has been no significant inward change in the way people feel about such topics. If you really want to get someone stirred up you have only to attack his religion or his politics, and sex, of course, is just a minefield. I would add another issue to this short list of dangerous topics: children. No issue is more contentious than the upbringing and education of children. For some reason just the mere mention of the word 'children' is enough to drive normally sane, sensible people into a frenzy. From that moment no theory is too nutty to be espoused and no statement too extreme to be proposed. Non-believers can expect pretty much the same treatment as heretics at the hands of the Inquisition. Beware when you argue about children!

The emotional content of an argument may often be of far more importance than the intellectual content and this is a fact that you ignore at your peril. Once hurt pride becomes an issue then it will prove the greatest of obstacles to getting a reasonable solution. In any argument in which you may be involved take great care to consider the effects of emotion.

Types of Argument

There are various types of argument, each with its own rules and methods.

The first major division is into public and private arguments. It is enormously important to decide whether you are arguing to convince an individual or whether you are merely using that person as a sounding board to help you convince others.

Private Arguments

Those arguments that take place between individuals, or in a small group of people with no audience listening, are clearly in the private category. The fact that such arguments are, by definition, carried on without an audience will have a profound effect on their shape. In a private argument, what is said will tend to be regarded as 'off the record' and people may well feel able to reveal feelings and opinions that they would hide from a wider audience. Inevitably a private argument will tend to concentrate on the personal aspects, even when matters of public importance are being discussed. Anecdotal evidence is very common in private arguments and people will frequently use their own experiences, and those of friends and relatives, to try to prove a case. They will often not be able or willing to see that just because Uncle Harry smoked forty cigarettes a day every day of his life from the age of eleven, and lived till he was eighty-seven, then that doesn't mean that it must be a load of rubbish that smoking gives you cancer.

Unless the participants are experienced arguers they will tend to make common mistakes such as confusing fact and opinion or quoting facts inaccurately. One of the strongest ploys you can use in private arguments is *Know-all* (see page 49), the simple ruse of knowing the facts and quoting them accurately. However, know-alls are never popular in any sphere and in arguments, where emotions are usually heightened, you risk making yourself unpopular by always knowing better. It may be wise to save this technique for occasions when it really matters.

Another important facet of private arguments is that the participants will take the outcome intensely personally and will frequently carry it over into other parts of their private life. You must have noticed how an argument with friends or colleagues can have repercussions quite out of proportion to the importance of the original disagreement. People have been known to refuse to speak to each other for days, months or even years because of some minor squabble that got out of control.

One of the troubles with private arguments is that they often serve as an outlet for underlying hostilities. In fact such an argument will frequently be engineered solely for the purpose of providing an outlet for past grudges. Even where the original argument is genuine, it is surprising how, when emotions become aroused, the placid surface of everyday behaviour gets completely disrupted. Once this has happened there are no limits to what can result. Look, for example, at what happened in the former Yugoslavia when some of the constituent peoples informed their Serb neighbours that they would like to go their own way and form independent states. This may at first appear to be a matter of politics but, when you listen to the stories of those involved, it becomes apparent that many of the grievances and hostilities had their origins in squabbles between neighbours that got completely out of hand. News reports all emphasized that people suffered atrocities that were committed not by a foreign army but, in many cases, by people they knew by name.

Public Arguments

On the other hand, in a public argument the participants are usually much more interested in the effect their words will have on the audience than in whether they can convince an opponent. Indeed, most of the people who argue in public (businessmen, lawyers, politicians, journalists) come into the category of professional arguers. Their whole career is conducted in an atmosphere of verbal strife and they attack or defend a point of view on a purely professional basis. It is not being cynical to suggest that frequently they do not personally believe in the point of view they are expressing with such eloquence at all. For the most part, 'ordinary' people do not come into contact with the world of professional public arguments. But it can happen. If it does you must be able to decide whether you should respond to your opponent as a person or merely as the mouthpiece of a particular point of view.

A public argument is necessarily more formal than a private one. Often it will be conducted according to specific rules and may even have some sort of umpire or chairperson to make sure the rules are kept. Even though tempers may flare they will rarely be allowed to get so out of hand that physical violence erupts. Additionally there is a penalty attached to letting oneself get carried away. The audience will take it as a sign of the weakness of one's case. There will also be some sort of timetable in operation and therefore unless you use your time skilfully you might inadvertently gloss over or forget important points. Once the argument is over, no matter how many witty retorts come to you on the way home, you will probably not get another chance. Most public arguments are one-off events where the quality of your performance on the day is just as important as whether you have right on your side.

Another feature of public arguments is that, in common with written arguments, they are almost always 'on the record', and usually there will be some kind of permanent record made in the form of notes, recorded on a paper and/or electronic document, or on audio or video tape or film. The tendency will therefore be for people to weigh their words carefully and avoid the sort of overly personal and dramatic statements that flourish in a purely private setting.

It is also likely that a lot more will be riding on the result of a public argument. Court cases, political debates (at both national and local level), public inquiries, and formal meetings of boards of governors are all the sorts of occasions where public arguments take place and where the results may well have far-reaching, long-term consequences. Even a debate on television, though it may appear to be little more than a piece of entertainment, will have an effect in moulding public opinion. Therefore a public argument is in all respects a much more serious affair than a private one.

Written Arguments

Almost all arguments can be carried on in writing but generally we reserve this method for our more formal disagreements. The reasons are obvious: anything you put in writing and send to someone enters the public domain and cannot be recalled. This has a number of implications, not least of which is that you can be held legally responsible for your words. Call a man a lying bastard to his face and you risk a split lip; write it down and you risk heavy damages for libel. However, in spite of the risks involved this method has considerable advantages that make it widely popular. The very fact that you and your opponent must measure your words and imagine them being read by a wider audience will inevitably raise the quality of debate. You will think twice about quoting evidence that can be retained and checked by an unknown number of third parties.

You will also, if you are prudent, remember that your words, if spoken hastily and unwisely, may return to haunt you. Anyone who remembers President Bush urging people to 'read my lips' while he promised no new taxes will also remember his immense discomfiture when he later broke that promise.

Written arguments have the other advantage of allowing you time for reflection and research before you reply to your opponent's latest onslaught. An argument conducted in writing will favour the conscientious researcher who pays attention to getting the details right but will penalize the person who relies on a ready wit to skate over the cracks in his reasoning.

Yet another reason for people favouring written arguments is that by putting your opponent at arm's length you remove his power to use some of the more aggressive techniques of argument. The written word forms a screen between you and the opponent that protects you from people who try to get their own way purely by force of personality. In fact, you may observe something interesting that often happens once people commit their arguments to writing. It is quite common to find rather ineffectual people who would not normally say boo to a goose transformed into lions once they are able to express themselves in writing. This can be a good thing if it enables people to get the fair hearing of which they would otherwise have been deprived. On the other hand there is the less pleasant phenomenon of the 'poisoned pen' in which people who seem quite affable suddenly reveal a talent for vituperation as soon as they are let loose with a pen and a sheet of paper.

The issue of emotion in written arguments is also interesting. People are on the whole less inclined to let themselves go when putting their thoughts down on paper. Many people resort to the old trick of writing two responses to their opponent. The first is the one where they really lash out and call him all the names they can think of. Then, having got that off their chest, they tear the first letter up and set about writing the calm, dignified response they are actually going to send. If you do not do this already it is a tactic well worth adopting.

In a written argument you have a chance, largely denied to you in face-to-face situations, to adopt a persona that may be quite at variance with your real character. Whereas in real life you might get easily flustered, stammer, go red in the face and forget the important details of your case (and we all do some of these things from time to time), once you enter the realm of written argument you can be as calm, suave and poised as you please – you have time to get it right. You may also choose to show the draft of your letter to a trusted friend or a paid advisor (such as your lawyer or accountant) and get the benefit of that advice before you send the final version. The great luxury of written arguments is that you can draft and redraft each document as many times as you wish until you get it exactly the way you want it.

Although written arguments have great advantages they also have dangers that you should bear in mind before embarking upon one. You should make quite sure that you are operating in a field where you know all the rules. You should not, for example, unless you have legal training, try to conduct a legal argument in writing. You may think that what you have said is straightforward and unambiguous but, in a legal context, words can take on meanings that they do not have in everyday speech. Also you will discover that lawyers are very practised at picking to pieces any argument presented to them. The only person likely to be able to stop them doing that is another lawyer. The rule here is to recognize your limitations and never let the joy of battle tempt you into playing out of your league.

If you are going to argue in writing you must be very strict with yourself and make sure you do not indulge in irrelevance and high-sounding waffle. Things you might just get away with when you speak can look awfully stupid when written down. Try to cut out words you do not need. Keep your sentences and paragraphs short and to the point. Make sure that your argument flows naturally and logically from your initial outline of the facts, through your proof, to what you hope is an inescapable conclusion.

Family Arguments

Kevin, a designer who used to do work for me, was in business with his younger brother. Things went pretty well for them for some years. They had a studio on the ground floor of their elderly mother's house and the whole family got on very well. Then the brother, Robert, got married to a French woman called Thérèse. Suddenly all hell was let loose. The new wife did not get on with the elder brother. The mother was drawn into the quarrel. The brothers stopped speaking. The rows became so frequent and so furious that the studio had to be partitioned to keep the warring factions apart. Finally they even had to have separate entrances to the house constructed. At the height of the mayhem a meeting was called with all the family members and their accountants and solicitors present. Things quickly got out of hand. Kevin, a rather easygoing soul most of the time, started to say something about trying to settle the whole mess reasonably when Thérèse bellowed at the top of her voice: 'What's reason got to do with it? A family is not a democracy!' It is a quotation worth remembering. It will remind you that family arguments are in a league of insanity all of their own.

An argument within the family is rarely concerned with the apparent subject matter. Most arguments start over something so banal as to be hardly worth considering, like whose turn it is to wash up, or whether someone remembered to lock the front door last night. If such an argument were to start outside the family it would probably be resolved quickly and possibly even amicably. However, families are different. When a little group of people lives together year in year out, often in a fairly confined space, frustrations are bound to build up. And because we are supposed to love our parents, partners and children no matter how badly they behave towards us, we often feel we have to suppress our resentment. No wonder explosions occur so often. When you see a family argument in full swing, that old statistic about people being most likely to get murdered by a member of their own family makes perfect sense. As the zoologist Desmond Morris observed, the interesting thing about people is not that they are so prone to violence but that for most of the time they manage to avoid it so well. It is worth mentioning that these remarks apply not just to traditional families but to other sorts of households, such as groups of students.

Furthermore, the very closeness of family relationships makes for high levels of emotion. Because our family members do love us we feel that we can exhibit to them a side of our personality that we have to keep hidden from the world at large. Sulky teenagers become even more morose with their parents, while frustrated husbands pick on their harassed wives and vice versa.

Family arguments are also in a class of their own in that they have almost nothing to do with reason, concern for the truth or even, in many cases, true self-interest. All these things are quite alien to the way people in families behave. Their main concern

21

will be with methods of manipulation (see page 94). They will use every trick in the book to cajole, blackmail or bamboozle their loved ones into behaving in the way they want. This process of manipulation will be the main purpose of the argument. The ostensible object will on most occasions be peripheral to the real aims of the arguers. In other words it doesn't matter in the slightest that you washed the car; what matters is that I made you wash it.

Manipulation has a bad name because it involves emotional dishonesty. People believe that it is not possible to have a good relationship with someone if you are not honest with them. However, families have their own internal structure and the practice of manipulation helps to maintain that structure. Many couples maintain a sort of emotional Punch and Judy relationship in which verbal assaults, followed by reconciliations, help to ensure that aggression is channelled safely and real violence never occurs.

There is little that we can do about this. Arguments of this sort, in moderation, help us to blow off steam and release the pressures under which we live. That is all to the good. The occasions when people lose control and a domestic argument turns into a blood bath, though they make sensational headlines, are mercifully few.

At the moment we are concerned with only one question: how do you win a family argument? Obviously different criteria apply from just about any other sort of argument. Within the family, just because you manage to make your spouse or child admit that it really was his or her turn to mow the lawn that does not mean you have in any meaningful sense won the argument. In fact, beating someone into submission (figuratively or literally) never counts as a win in such circumstances. Winning is only achieved by an outcome that will help the family to continue functioning effectively. A bloody good row in which all parties give vent to their suppressed anger can be a win for everybody involved if it is followed by a genuine reconciliation. 'Say what you like but never go to bed mad,' is the best advice anyone can follow in a family row.

Arguments and the Gender Gap

When considering the types of arguments in which people indulge I thought it might be interesting to consider whether women argue differently from men. Perhaps my whole perspective on argument was exclusively male and was therefore blinding me to a side of the subject that women would find obvious. I started by asking friends and colleagues what they thought. Almost without exception they claimed that women would argue differently with members of their own sex than with men. They accepted that in mixed company women might well be pressured into emulating a male style of argument but, among themselves, they would be far more reasonable. A lot of well-worn prejudices started to appear. Men felt that women were more inclined to argue from a purely emotional point of view while they, of course, were practical, hard-headed chaps who seldom let emotion rule their reason. Strangely, women felt something similar about themselves. However, they preferred to put it a different way and used words like 'feeling', 'intuition', and 'consensus'. They, you will be unsurprised to hear, were not impressed by the men's claims to be more reasonable. They felt that they were themselves perfectly reasonable but possessed some ill-defined extra quality that men could never quite grasp.

All this was getting a bit subjective so I made a point during my periods of argument-spotting of noticing the differences between the sexes. I found none. It soon became quite obvious that women could be just as emotional, practical, reasonable, bloody-minded, truthful, deceitful, and so on, as men. I still cannot persuade my friends that this is true.

Children's Arguments

If you want to become a proficient arguer you could do no better than to start by observing children's arguments. Young children have a natural mastery of some unsophisticated but deadly effective techniques. Their main strength is that they are dedicated wholeheartedly and unselfconsciously to getting their own way. They do not yet suffer the pangs of adult conscience. Even when they get just a little older and know (intellectually) that they should consider what other people want, they are very good at pushing that thought to one side.

The first childhood technique is the *Chinese Water Torture* (see page 46). The simple assertion 'I want . . . ' repeated incessantly will often overcome the resistance of even the most strong-minded adult. Children seem to know the effectiveness of this technique by instinct. It is, after all, only an extension of the behaviour of the baby that cries and cries and cries until it gets the attention it wants. The great mistake we make as adults is to overlook the simplicities of childhood and concentrate on what we think of as more sophisticated behaviour. It is often the simplest ploys that win.

Another interesting facet of young children's arguments is that they may find it hard to use reason but this never stops them from arguing vigorously and effectively. They will happily invent 'facts' that suit their case and will quote 'authorities' to back them up. The fact that such subterfuges can be seen through so easily when used by children should make us wary of adults who also resort to them. Is the child who says, 'It's true because my dad told me so,' doing anything so very different from the lawyer who calls an 'expert' witness?

Listening to children argue is one of the best ways to observe how the process works. It cuts out all the sanctimonious flim-flam that adults use to justify their actions and concentrates on the all-important, 'I want.'

Aggressive Arguments

Sometimes arguments become violent. Strictly speaking, ugly incidents of this sort are not really arguments at all. An aggressive argument is just a fight looking for an excuse to happen. The scenario is common enough. For example, two men in a hurry to catch the same underground train collide as they rush for the doors. In their struggle to be first on board they push and shove while the doors hiss shut and the train departs without them. The scene is now set for an aggressive argument. The younger man snarls an audible obscenity at the older who says, 'I beg your pardon, would you mind repeating that?' 'Yeah, I said you're a ******!' There now follows a series of exchanges in which each man tries to get the other either to cross the line between verbal and physical aggression or to back off. This may last quite some time or it may explode into a fist fight straight away. In either case the men are not really arguing in any real sense, they are merely indulging in what, in lower primates, would be described as a threat display. The trouble with situations like this is that both parties become locked into the situation with no possibility of a dignified retreat. If neither backs down but, even so, they are unwilling to fight, they will go into a slow retreat whilst glaring at each other and exchanging the sort of language your mother told you never to use. Anyone trying to intervene and make them see reason is, of course, in danger of becoming the focus for their anger.

'Every Question Has Two Sides'

It was a lawyer in ancient Greece called Protagoras who usually gets the credit for the idea that there are two sides to every question. But is it true? If so, it is a matter of some importance to anyone considering the subject of argument. For if we accept his notion, all ideas of right and wrong go straight out the window and we are left with nothing but a sort of wishy-washy relativism in which any argument consists of no more than the opinions of the arguers.

Certainly much of our daily experience seems to support Protagoras' view. We constantly hear an argument advanced, and may even be quite convinced by it, only to come across an equally convincing counter-argument that leaves us again in doubt. The most obvious case is that of political debate in which the tide of argument constantly ebbs and flows without ever seeming to reach any firm conclusions. An even better example is that of economic policy. All informed adults have tried to make some sense of economics. They may have listened to the experts in an attempt to understand the situation only to give up in disgust when they discover that, for every expert who proposes one theory, there is another who holds just as firmly to the opposite view.

Elsewhere in this book I have laid great stress upon getting your facts straight. Facts, however, are slippery little devils and have a habit of jumping about in a surprising fashion. Take this little exchange between my friend Liam and me.

'Do you know,' said Liam, 'that the Irish were the only people in Europe never to persecute the Jews?'

'Really?' I was impressed. 'Is that because of your easygoing Celtic tolerance?'

'Not at all. It was our Catholic bigotry. We just never let 'em in!'

The point is that Fact 1 (assuming it is true) gives one impression and could be quoted to bolster a case for Irish tolerance. Fact 2, when revealed, gives an entirely different impression and could be used to make an almost opposite case.

This is not an abstract issue. It has great relevance to all our lives. What is more, in recent times the tendency to believe that opposing views are merely alternative, and equally valid, opinions has become so strong that many people are genuinely confused about whether they can really hold any point of view at all.

This confusion has been made immeasurably worse by the advent of political correctness. No one with any degree of sensitivity would seriously be in favour of offending disabled people by calling them 'cripples' or hurting the feelings of gay people by dubbing them 'bent'. Likewise we are becoming more aware of issues of gender, race and age where a thoughtless remark might give offence. However, this recent outbreak of sensitivity raises its own problems. In the first place the new PC terms are often clumsy and risible. It seems perfectly fair to refer to 'people with Downs Syndrome' instead of 'mongols', but can we really keep a straight face while talking of the 'vertically challenged'? Yet who nowadays would dare mention midgets?

Far more serious is the fact that an increasing number of issues do not admit debate because to discuss them seriously would be a breach of PC. For example, can black people be guilty of racial intolerance? It would not be hard to cite incidents from all over the world to back up such a proposition, but the PC answer is a flat 'No'. This poses a serious problem. As soon as it is not acceptable to voice unpopular views, even if the censors think they are acting from worthy motives, democracy is endangered. Argument not only provides an emotional safety valve in letting people blow off steam without resorting to violence, it also ensures the health of society by letting even the most unacceptable views be heard.

Our school English teacher, who hailed from a time when PC would have been unintelligible to almost everyone, was a firm believer in developing one's powers of argument. He absolutely insisted on the intellectual value of discussion and made us practise sharpening our wits on each other by holding regular classroom debates. Furthermore he kept a careful note of our opinions and beliefs and would take a great pleasure in casting each of us in a role to which we were fundamentally opposed. He forced convinced Socialists to defend Tory policies and made bigots of the truest blue argue for the abolition of immigration controls. This was not done from malice but from a deeply held conviction that we should be able to defend our corner in any battle of wits. His fervour in this respect knew no bounds and reached its summit when he prevailed upon a boy called Solomons to assume the role of Hitler and defend his new Nazi party against another boy representing the flabby democrats of the Weimar Republic. These days the national Press would get wind of such an episode and the teacher would be lucky not to be flung out on his ear. However, those were more robust times and he expected us to make the most of the opportunities to hone our intellects to the required razor-like sharpness. Solomons was no slouch when it came to a debate and he wiped the floor with his democratic opponent.

The trouble is that argument is such a very useful tool and, in the hands of an expert, can convince us of almost anything. Even when you think you have an issue nicely nailed down it is quite possible for someone to come along and upset your cherished opinion.

Take, for example, something you might think is pretty safe territory. Everyone knows that snack foods such as crisps and chips are bad for children, don't they? In these health-conscious times it is almost an article of religion for many middle-class parents. Now listen to what Professor Donald J. Naismith of the Department of Nutrition and Dietetics at King's College, University of London had to say in the matter in a letter to *The Independent* in January, 1994:

Sir: Your article ('Store-war price cuts "promote junk food"', 11 January) reports the attack by the Food Commission on the misguided, if not cynical, policy of the supermarkets in discounting so-called junk foods in preference to 'healthy' foods. The foods listed are particularly popular among children, who have very distinct food preferences and aversions which, as most parents discover, are abandoned with the onset of maturity. Cutting the cost of food for children is surely not a policy to be deplored.

The prevalence of obesity in children is at present around 5 per cent. The vast majority are thus not obese, and an increasing proportion of children are showing poor growth and low body weight resulting simply from inadequate intake of energy (not protein or vitamins and minerals). The cause is poverty. Since energy is the major determinant of growth, the choice of cheap energy-dense foods (such as chips) is to be commended. Cutting the price of high-fibre low-calorie fruits and vegetables would be of little help.

The claim that the foods listed are 'inferior' is a very misleading one. Inferior to what? Hamburgers made from top-quality steak and fish fingers made from whole cod (unmashed) could be of higher nutritional value but would undoubtedly cost a great deal more. Is a glass of mineral water superior to a can of soft drink (140 calories)? Is an apple (47 calories) superior to a bag of crisps (164 calories) which, incidentally, provides not only more fibre than an apple but also more of the antioxidant vitamins C and E and is the richest common dietary source of potassium, a mineral, thought to prevent the development of hypertension.

People are receptive to health education that acknowledges the socio-economic factors that limit food choice and is couched in terms that are easily understood. The layman may be baffled by the chemistry of his dietary fats but is able to tell his flora from his fauna. Coercion by pricing is unlikely to bring about a change in eating habits, even among the adult population, and the dogmatic approach favoured by the Food Commission generates resentment, not enlightenment.

Should the supermarkets decide, however, to cut the cost of items believed to have a role in the prevention of atherosclerosis, then may I suggest they begin with table wines?

Where does all this leave us? Are there no areas that are beyond dispute? Is there no ultimate truth at which we can arrive? Is everything just a quicksand of endlessly shifting opinion? I was discussing this point with a younger friend of a scientific bent who was quick to point out that at least scientific truths are beyond dispute. 'Really?' I said. 'But surely scientists are disagreeing with each other constantly and are regularly over-turning theories that most people had come to accept as fact?'

'Oh, of course,' said my friend, 'but there are some areas where we are now quite sure of the truth. For example, we know now that the Earth is round and goes around the Sun. Nothing will ever change that because we have proved it beyond any shadow of doubt.'

It was an interesting thought. Surely he was quite right and, if so, then there are incontrovertible facts and Protagoras was quite wrong. Some questions can be settled so that they no longer have two sides.

I asked the scientist Brian J. Ford about it. He has examined such questions in several of his books, and he has a surprising view on the way we perceive scientific argument. What about the now-disproved theory that the earth was flat? Surely the discovery of the fact that the world was a sphere was the end of the matter?

'Absolutely not,' he told me. 'The notion of the world being a sphere did not last long. The first challenge in that conven-tion was when we realized the earth is flattened and slightly ovoid. It isn't a sphere at all, but an oblate spheroid. Then it turned out there was a slight bulge on one side. Now that we have satellite measurements, we realize that the supposedly rounded contour of the earth has hollows and lumps. There are some places where the sea-level is unnaturally raised, and others where it sinks into a slight depression. The modern view of the earth is oblate, but with many slight hills and hollows all round it. It looks more like a battered grapefruit than a sphere.'

Is it possible that some of the old scientific views have some truth in them still? Brian J. Ford thinks that they do.

'The first microscopists reasoned that there must be an entire human in the head of a sperm,' he said. This was the so-called homunculus theory. In modern terms it seems very out of date and almost mediaeval. 'But it was right, after all,' Brian explains. 'Although it seems fanciful, the argument that lay behind it was perfectly sound. We now know that they were right all along – there is a human inside the head of a sperm. It may be in encoded form, as DNA, but the human is there all right, just as those sages predicted. Sometimes we should realise that there is more sense than nonsense in an early scientific idea. There are many lessons science has yet to learn from arguments of the past.'

So it seems increasingly as if Protagoras had it right after all. This may be bad news for seekers after truth but it is very good news for arguers. What it means is that, as long as you are ingenious enough, you can often keep an argument going indefinitely.

At this point we are in serious danger of subsiding into a dreadful quicksand of opinion and contradictory fact. Worst of all, the entire subject of argument could sink up to its neck in issues of philosophy. Where, we sigh to ourselves sadly, does the cup end and the saucer begin? Just at this point, in steps PC Bludge. 'Do you mind telling me where you were at 7.30 last Friday evening, sir?' Not a very interesting question but one that demands a factual answer. One can imagine that Bludge would not take kindly to an answer that began, 'Well, officer, it all depends what you mean by "where". I mean, "where" relative to what?'

There are, after all, big facts and little facts. The big ones may

32

be tricky and capable of more than one interpretation but the little ones can be nailed down with some degree of precision. For example, if you ask someone, 'Who are you?' you would not be satisfied with the reply, 'Ah, that's just what I was wondering myself!' A name is required. Having been given that name you would probably be able to check whether it was genuine or not. Philosophical issues would not be involved.

Later in the book I shall make much of the necessity of getting your facts straight and insisting that an opponent does likewise. While I am well aware that facts have their problems there is still no substitute for getting the best and most accurate information you can to back up your arguments. It is the ammunition that will help you win every war.

Arguments in Other Cultures

This book was written primarily from an Anglo-American perspective. My comments apply principally to the inhabitants of the British Isles and, to a slightly lesser extent, to those of the USA.

Normally when you start to argue with someone you will be in a position where, even if you are not aware of it, you agree about far more things than you disagree about. These things are the cultural influences that you have in common.

First, you are, literally, talking the same language and that makes linguistic misunderstandings less likely. Second, you share a whole culture and all your cultural references will be mutually understandable. Third, you will play the argument game by the same rules – you will agree about what is fair play, you will both be aware of what you can and can't say without appearing rude, and you will both recognize the point at which argument changes from discussion to aggression.

When you start to argue with people from other cultures, all these conventions that you understand so well when dealing with your own people break down completely. Words change their meaning, gestures are misunderstood, important nuances of meaning are lost. It's like driving a car in a thick fog, and the crashes can be just as disastrous.

Some years ago a British man was on a camping holiday in France with his father. One night the father was brutally murdered and the French police suspected the son. During interrogation they asked him if he and his father had had '*un discussion*' the evening before the murder. He readily agreed that they had spent the whole evening in discussion, quite unaware that in French the word can be used to mean a row.

Unfortunately there are so many pitfalls of this sort that it would take an encyclopaedia to list them all. However, there are some vital differences that you must bear in mind when arguing with people of other cultures.

The British and, to a lesser extent, the Americans find argument rude and, at least in theory, try to avoid it where possible. In Britain you regularly hear people lying their heads off in an attempt to be agreeable and avoid an argument. Internationally what we would call our natural tact has given us a reputation for perfidy. Yes, it's true! They don't trust us! To foreign ears that British obliqueness, cleverly designed to avoid giving offence, comes across as a sneaky attempt to evade the issue. Even our first cousins, the Americans, believe that to be true. Why do you think that villains in American television programmes so often have British accents?

If misunderstandings can arise between people who are as closely related as the British and Americans, what hope is there when we argue with real foreigners? For, however much we may feel that Americans are kindred spirits, the truth is that in argument we have quite different styles. When the British negotiate they tend to adopt a rather informal style. Even important deals are frequently done on the strength of nothing more than a verbal agreement. In America they are much keener on lawyers and contracts. And this leads to a problem immediately. It is not that the British don't believe in legal formalities, but to insist on them in the wrong circumstances looks very much as if you don't trust the other party. Even worse, you may give the impression that you want to get the deal sealed quickly because you have just pulled a fast one and hope that your opponent won't notice until after he's signed.

What is more, the custom in Britain is to go for a mutually satisfactory agreement. A compromise is still the most likely outcome of any British argument, especially a negotiation. Attempting to beat your opponent into the dirt and then stomp all over him is not common practice. Try doing business in the USA and you will be in for a surprise. 'This is my final position,' is a phrase that will be familiar to anyone who has crossed the pond on business. Of course, they don't mean it or they would never reach any agreements at all. The problem is that they sound as if they mean it and the British vocabulary of argument does not contain the right words to break the blockade. They expect you to fight for what you want. A much more aggressive style of argument than is acceptable at home is vital if you want to get anywhere in the USA. For them, to misquote Clausewitz, the Prussian military strategist, business is war carried on by other means.

Interestingly, the aggressive attitude to argument in America is noticeable chiefly in the business field and much less so in daily life. This in itself creates confusion because British visitors cannot readily understand why those nice guys who are usually so much friendlier and more sociable than Britishers at home turn into such bastards as soon as they put on a suit. Suspicions of duplicity are immediately aroused.

Aggressiveness in argument is very common in many other countries and is not considered to be rude. The French, who enjoy argument as a national pastime, have something called *la gueulade* (*la gueule* is a coarse word for 'face' and is normally reserved for animals unless you are looking for a punch in the teeth). As far as I can make out, *la gueulade* involves being provocatively rude to someone, often a complete stranger, in the hope of striking up an argument that will eventually give both parties great enjoyment. The idea of argument as a pastime does not strike much of a chord with the British. Of course, in Britain it is all right to discuss controversial matters but it is done with the usual obliqueness and with one eye kept shrewdly on your opponent's sensibilities. The Gallic equivalent looks to us about as inviting as a bout between lady mud wrestlers.

All this plain speaking contrasts starkly with customs in some oriental countries where any form of opponent dissent constitutes a deadly insult. When I lived in Thailand, one of the first things my friends taught me about was 'the yes that means no'. A question like, 'Would you like to come to my party next Friday?' must always be answered in the affirmative even if you have a perfectly good excuse for not attending. 'I'm sorry but my wife was run over and I have to go to the funeral' is not an acceptable excuse. There are no acceptable excuses. However, there are polite formulas you can use, while thanking your would-be host warmly for inviting you and expressing your keen anticipation of the great event, which will warn him not to set an extra place for you.

In a similar vein, the Thais find it extremely hard to express disagreement without giving offence. Unlike westerners they are deprived of a whole armoury of brusque remarks that indicate to people that you are starting to get annoyed with them. One of their favourite expressions is *chai yen* or 'cool heart'. It involves keeping your temper in even the most trying of circumstances and is considered a highly desirable characteristic. Unfortunately when *chai yen* finally cracks, and they are only human so eventually it does crack, the results can be frightening. On one memorable occasion some students were expressing their discontent with the status quo by hanging the Crown Prince in effigy. In the west their behaviour would have invited some sharp comments at most. However, such behaviour would have violated *chai yen*. Eventually the bystanders got to the end of their tether and beat the offenders to death with some folding seats that happened to be lying nearby.

The Japanese also have some problems with being misunderstood by westerners. There is a memorable true story of a British girl boarding with a Japanese family while pursuing her studies in Tokyo. One day the family decided that it was time to put up the rent. Naturally they summoned the girl and, in polite Japanese style, offered to lower the rent. She, being an ignorant westerner, took their offer at face value and accepted it gratefully. Their fury knew no bounds and it was ages before the poor girl found out what she had done and managed to put it right.

In Japan if you want to make any remark that might possibly be construed as criticism you must always start off by taking the blame yourself. A British engineering lecturer who had been hired to instruct Japanese workers in the operation of new machinery ended his discourse with the customary, 'Any questions?'. Complete silence was accompanied by the uncomfortable shuffling of feet. The lecturer was nonplussed. He had been brought over at considerable expense to the company to explain complicated machinery and unless they asked him questions they would never be able to work it. In desperation he asked the translator for advice. 'Ah,' said the young man knowingly, 'you asked the wrong way. You must say, "I am sure I have explained this very badly and if there are any points I could make clearer please tell me what they are."' The rephrased question brought the desired results.

So where does all this leave us? It is simply not feasible for us to become expert on all the national peculiarities of every person with whom we might possibly have an argument. However, it is when dealing with people from another cultural background that it becomes most important to try to stand in your opponent's shoes. Elsewhere in this book I have pointed out that looking too closely at an argument through your opponent's eyes may lead you to weaken your resolve. However, when dealing with people whose culture you do not share you have no choice. Unless you make some attempt to find common ground you will be quite unable to conduct any argument at all. With the good old safety valve of argument firmly shut, frustration will quickly build up on both sides and an ugly and unproductive quarrel will quickly ensue.

Unfortunately many people are not very open to unfamiliar cultural influences. It is much easier to stick uncomplimentary labels on people than to try to understand what makes them tick. Thus many a Britisher is convinced that the French are pompous, the Germans hidebound, the Italians over-excitable, and so on.

It really does pay to try to get inside the skin of your foreign opponent. It may even change the character of your argument altogether. For instance, I am reliably informed by my

Francophile friends that *la gueulade*, which sounds exactly to an English ear like a deadly insult, is intended to pave the way for a discussion (in the English sense of the word). The aim is, by being quite deliberately controversial, to initiate the sort of prolonged debate of which the French are so fond.

Similarly, I used to be incensed when Germans stopped us in the street and commented adversely on the way we were treating our children ('Not dressed warmly enough. You should have more sense!'). My (German) wife pointed out that, at least in their own eyes, they were just being helpful. The expected response was a polite expression of gratitude, not a swift kick to the ankle.

If you are going to a foreign country it will pay you to learn how the locals argue and what they really mean by it. You should bear in mind that the over-restrained British attitude probably strikes them as incomprehensible (unless, of course, they are Orientals in which case they may see you as rude and pushy). Wherever possible you should pick the brains of other British people who know the country in question and find out what the score is. Do people expect you to haggle or is it regarded as rude? Are you allowed to express open disagreement or is that equivalent to a declaration of war? Can you describe your feelings openly or must you dress them up in polite formulas to make them acceptable. A little research will make all the difference.

Victories Are Not Solutions

The whole purpose of this book is to teach you how to win arguments but it may be as well to consider for a moment just what we mean by that. What do we really hope to gain by arguing? This question is likely to have more than one answer depending upon the circumstances. There are two basic outcomes we may hope for: a moral victory or a material gain. The moral victory may sound noble but, in most circumstances, it is quite the opposite. We embark on many arguments with no aim other than to inflict a humiliation on our opponent. When this is the case this aim will take precedence over all else and will certainly not be tempered by minor considerations like truth, justice or even self-interest. Arguments bred of deep feelings of hostility will focus entirely upon the expression of those feelings regardless of the consequences. A 'win' will only be achieved by making an opponent back off, climb down, or look foolish in front of others. On the other hand, in cases where a material gain is our object, what we regard as 'winning' may become altogether more complicated. It is entirely possible that in these circumstances a win will look unspectacular. It may even look suspiciously like a defeat. There is a saying among diplomats that diplomacy is about achieving results not winning arguments. You may, for example, grab at a good compromise that gives you more than you hoped for even though it falls far short of what would appear to be a victory over your opponents. John Hume, the SDLP Member of Parliament and one of the authors of the peace talks in Northern Ireland, was asked at one juncture in the talks who had 'won' a particular point. His reply was worth remembering: 'For us,' he said, 'victories are not solutions.'

If material gain is your object you must keep that gain firmly in sight and resist the temptation to rub your opponent's nose in the dirt. You may even choose to win by appearing to 'lose' the argument yourself. The case of the wife who regularly wins by letting her husband believe that all the good ideas are his own has become a stock comedy situation and, like all such comedy classics, it has a lot of truth in it. Losing, done skilfully, can be winning.

There are other sorts of victory to which we may aspire. If, for example, what started as an argument deepens until it becomes a mutual exploration in which the truth is sought then that is a true victory. Similarly if an argument that started with people hoping to humiliate each other results in enough steam being let off for them to settle their differences amicably, that too is a victory.

When Not to Argue

Nothing is simpler than starting an argument: we feel frustrated and desperately keen to persuade someone of our viewpoint and we argue. It is so much part of our culture that we do not have to give it a moment's consideration. But are there occasions when it would be better not to bother? Here are a few you might like to consider.

First, it is pointless arguing with the wrong person. How many times have you heard dissatisfied customers giving some unfortunate sales assistant or office receptionist hell? Quite often the problem is not that the assistant has been slow, stupid or uncooperative but that the management is in some way at fault. Taking your frustrations out on the wrong person, though understandable, is a bad move. First, it is unjust and you will probably hate yourself later. Second, if and when you eventually reach the right person to receive your wrath you will have put him on his guard against you and put yourself at least partly in the wrong by your aggressive behaviour.

There are a number of other bad wickets on which you should refuse to play. A particularly important one is when there is a good chance that the argument may lead to violence. Our rule is that argument is there to serve as a safety valve to prevent violence not as a preparation for it. Aggressive arguments (see page 62) should be avoided at all costs.

Another classic argument you should avoid is the one you are bound to lose. If you know that, no matter what you say, your opponent will not be persuaded then you should consider whether it is worth saying it in the first place. That is not to say that you should never stick up for an issue of principle against stiff opposition. However, bear in mind that once you have started an argument you will inevitably strengthen your opponent's resolve. If, on the other hand, you refrain from open opposition you are still free to try other, less obvious tactics like, for example, *Sir Humphrey* (see page 93). The glaring exception to this is when you are involved in a public argument. In this case you do not care about the obduracy of your opponent but about the malleability of the audience.

The cost of winning an argument should also be counted before you start. Being right is nice and being victorious is nicer, but how much are you willing to pay? Take, for example, a typical office squabble with your boss. You may feel, rightly, that he is yet again being unfair and stupid. But how far do you want to take it? An argument is not over just because the participants run out of things to say. The consequences can linger for days, months, even years. Before you get deep into an argument just pause to reckon up the probable cost. If it is too high you can avoid paying by simply keeping your mouth shut.

Summary

- Remember that an argument is not the same as a negotiation. In a negotiation, the aim is to reach an agreement; in an argument, the aim is to win.
- Have confidence in the justice of your own argument.
- Your arguments will receive a more sympathetic hearing if you show a concern for the truth. But don't expect to find such a concern in your opponent.
- Consider what your opponent stands to gain from winning the argument, and understand your own motives.
- Weigh the advantage you stand to gain by winning the argument against the costs involved.
- Be aware of the extent to which you and your opponent may be emotionally involved in an argument, and guard against your emotions getting the upper hand.
- Know your facts, but don't be too much of a know-all in situations where it is not necessary or appropriate.
- In a public argument, don't let yourself get carried away; weigh your words, make sure you get your points across clearly in the time allotted to you, and remember that you may be recorded.
- Do your research thoroughly before embarking on a written argument. Make written arguments brief and to the point, check your words thoroughly and seek expert advice if necessary.
- Don't conduct a legal argument in writing unless you have legal training.
- In a family argument, 'Say what you like but never go to bed mad.'
- Observe children's arguments; remember that it is often the simplest ploys that win.
- Gather well-documented facts to support your argument, but be aware that facts can be interpreted in different ways.
- When arguing with someone from a different cultural

background, be aware of possible stylistic differences. Do some research when you travel abroad.

- Don't attempt to argue with the wrong person. Seek out the right person.
- Avoid aggressive arguments.
- Don't start a private argument that you cannot possibly win.

CHAPTER TWO

Things You Can Do To Win

So far we have talked about argument in general terms. This will, I hope, have provided some interesting background, but now comes the real meat of the book. This chapter looks specifically at what you do to win an argument.

I have made the list of tactics as comprehensive as possible and included every technique that could possibly be of use. Some of the tactics are undoubtedly unethical or even downright immoral but I make no excuse for including them in the list. Whether you choose to use them yourself will be a personal decision. However, others may decide to use them against you and it is important that you be prepared for any eventuality.

Tactics do not exist in isolation. They are often combined to form a complete strategy of argument. When you argue you should aim to have not just one tactic up your sleeve but a planned strategy that gives you options that you can pursue if your first attempt goes wrong. Also you must consider all the surrounding circumstances of the argument, such as time, place and ambience (see Chapter 3).

First, let's look at the list. I have unashamedly borrowed the technique of the late Eric Berne whose book *Games People Play* made such a great contribution to the public's understanding of transactional analysis. The various tactics used in arguing have been given nicknames and treated as though they were elements in a game. As with Dr Berne's work this is not an attempt to trivialize something that should be treated seriously; it is rather an attempt to make what follows more interesting and memorable. It is important that you should be able to recall what you have learned about argument at the crucial time when you are in a corner and under stress.

Tactics come in several basic styles: offensive, defensive and manipulative. We shall take these groups in order.

Offensive Tactics

Chinese Water Torture

As its name implies, this involves getting your way by a persistence reminiscent of the drip, drip, drip of the fabled Chinese torture. Children are the acknowledged past masters of this technique and every parent will shamefacedly admit to having given in as a result of persistent and apparently never-ending nagging. No amount of patient reasoning will prevail against the child who whines incessantly, 'But I want an ice cream!' However, adults do it too. Most grown-up people find it a little undignified to go on and on trying to get their own way in the face of determined opposition. But it is just this squeamishness that makes *Chinese Water Torture* such a devastatingly effective technique. Those who adopt it have the single-mindedness not to care what other people think of them. All they want is to win the argument. Nothing else matters and nothing will deflect them from their one aim. A true story will make the point.

George, an old friend and the most persistently successful (or should that be 'successfully persistent'?) arguer I have ever come across, used to work in the printing trade. Being an ingenious and resourceful man he saw the advantages of computer typesetting in the days when most people were still using hot metal. He was a senior manager in his company and therefore he drew his bosses' attention to the new developments and suggested that they should quickly invest in new equipment and steal a march on their rivals. He got a cool reception. The investment needed was large and, anyway, it was just a passing fad wasn't it? George persisted but got nowhere. He waited a while and raised the subject again. Still nothing would persuade the owners of the company to invest in new technology. After some time George's persistence got on everyone's nerves. While the directors were having a board meeting they took the opportunity to call him in and warn him not to raise the subject again. Ever. Half an hour later there was a tap on the boardroom door and George appeared. 'You know that subject you told me not to mention again? Well, I'm raising it.' In sheer exasperation they told him to go and buy the equipment.

Of course, the story could have worked out quite differently. Many employers would have run out of patience and given George the sack. One of the marks of a good arguer is the ability to judge accurately the mood of his opponent.

The *Chinese Water Torture*, as used by adults, has a number of distinct variations. One involves a single marathon argument in which you try simply to outlast your opponent. There is more than one way to do this. In the first you follow the advice of Robert Owen (the Welsh educational and social reformer): 'Never argue, just repeat your assertion'. This, however, may become tedious and look as if you lack invention. The second, more difficult method is to filibuster until your opponent gets fed up. This requires considerable powers of oratory and a sound knowledge of your subject. There is a third way that has enjoyed considerable success. In this you do not try to argue with your opponent over the issues that actually divide you. Instead you digress endlessly and talk about a whole range of subjects, the duller the better, that have little or nothing to do with the subject under discussion. With luck your opponent eventually gives up and leaves you victorious.

During the 1950s and 1960s, when there was a great growth of left-wing activism, one technique used to great effect by certain Communist sympathizers was to join an organization, a trade union for example, attend its meetings and monopolize the discussion with endless irrelevancies, points of order, and petty matters that were of no importance and held no interest for the majority of people present. Eventually everyone but the most dedicated opponents would get bored and sneak out of the meeting, whereupon the leftists, now being comfortably in a majority, would introduce their political agenda and get down to the real business of the meeting.

George was adept at a more refined version of the technique that is called *Daruma* after the Japanese Buddhist sage of that name. If you have ever seen one of those curious little weighted Japanese dolls that jump up every time they are knocked over, you will immediately understand how this method works. George simply never accepted that an argument had ended until he had won it. Although I have defeated him in arguments on a number of occasions he would always wait a few days and then start again. If I attempted to remind him that we had already had the conversation he would have conveniently forgotten about it.

Of all the techniques for winning arguments the *Chinese*

Water Torture is by far the most devastatingly effective. If you were to be limited to mastering only one tactic this would, without doubt, be the one. However, it is not as easy as it sounds. In order to outlast your opponent you must cultivate a degree of sheer bloody-mindedness that will not come naturally to you. The moment you think to yourself, 'Who cares?' you will have lost the argument.

There is one other point to remember in connection with this technique. It only works if there is no time limit imposed upon the argument. If, for example, you are arguing on a public platform, or in a television studio, there will be an arbitrary limit to how long you can go on. Also, though you may try to hog the argument and prevent your opponent from getting a proper say, there may well be some third party, a chairperson for example, who sees to it that a fair balance is maintained. The *Chinese Water Torture* will not prevail in swift encounters that depend on quick wits or keenly argued logic.

Know-all

My old friend David Hall, doyen of the library of London University's School of Asian and African Studies, used to enjoy many a friendly wrangle with me to while away the long hours spent commuting to London. On occasions when I seemed to be getting the better of the argument he would draw himself to his full height and, looking suitably magisterial, intone in his huffiest voice, 'Well, if you're simply going to cloud the issue with facts I shan't bother to argue with you.' Thus we come to another powerful winning technique: knowing your stuff.

If you listen to many arguments you will quickly notice how many people have very little grasp of the facts. They depend mainly on their own prejudices and inclinations. To these they will add selectively from bits and pieces they have read, or television and radio programmes they have listened to. However, you can safely bet that their knowledge of the facts is sketchy at best, and probably most of their so-called facts are downright wrong.

Someone who has the patience to commit facts, figures, names and dates to memory is in a very powerful position to win arguments. If you watch politicians at work you will see what I mean. You will very rarely see them caught out on a matter of fact, no matter how wrong-headed their interpretation of that fact may be. Of course, they have an advantage over you in that they have paid researchers to look up the answers for them! But the principle remains the same. You must be sure of your facts. Nothing, but nothing, is more destructive to your case than to be caught out in an error of fact. If you want to be taken seriously you must have the facts straight. What is more, you must be able to quote the source of your facts. It is no good saying, 'I read a report the other day that said two glasses of red wine a day would help protect you from heart attacks'. This is far too vague and woolly. You must be able to say, 'In the February 1994 issue of *The Lancet*, Dr Justin Thyme from St Swithin's Hospital published a report stating that, in a study carried out on a sample of 1600 men over the age of 50, it was discovered that those who had regularly drunk two glasses of red wine a day were 60 per cent less likely to suffer a heart attack than non-drinkers of the same age.' See how impressive that sounds? Of course, I made these 'facts' up. For the technique to work you must have genuine information. Be prepared, however, for your opponent to come up with another report that makes opposing claims (it is never hard to find experts who disagree with each other). With facts of your own you will at least be in a position to try to discredit your opponents' facts. If you have none to offer you have lost straight away.

The glaring disadvantage of playing *Know-all* is that it really is a lot of hard work. If you are going to do it regularly you need to put in a lot of study time and have an excellent memory for details. Not everyone can do this. Probably no one can be so well prepared that he can have all the facts and figures ready for every argument in which he is likely to be involved.

Let us assume that you have the time and opportunity to amass factual evidence before you enter into an argument. Your next task is to marshal your facts in an orderly fashion. Your argument must flow logically from one point to another and arrive, without digression, at your chosen destination. Never use an argument as a chance to think aloud and re-examine the evidence. It shows that you have not given the subject sufficient thought and are still trying to make up your own mind. It's not very persuasive to an opponent. Be ruthless with yourself in cutting out anything that smacks of digression. If possible, give your argument a dry run with a friend before you try it out for real. Get someone whose abilities you respect to try to pick holes in your case.

It is very important to distinguish between fact and opinion. This may seem straightforward but it is often a source of confusion. There is nothing wrong with stating an opinion in an argument as long as you are quite clear what you are doing. If you have some special expertise in the field about which you are talking then your opinion may very well carry weight with your opponent. However, if you are merely parroting something you have heard elsewhere that confirms your own prejudices, the force of your argument will be much less. Statements that begin, 'Everybody knows . . . ' are opinions, not facts. What everybody knows, or what they believe they know, is apt to change from time to time and may have little to do with fact. At one time everyone knew the Earth was flat. Of course, that was a long time ago and people are more sophisticated now, aren't they? Probably not. I can remember a time when many people thought they 'knew' that black people were stupid, dirty and lazy. Many people assumed these to be indisputable facts and would have been shocked immeasurably if you had told them that thirty or forty years later people would hotly dispute such 'facts'. A fact is only a fact when it can be backed up by hard evidence. Even then there are problems.

In modern times many issues have become so complicated that even people who try to keep abreast of the facts may have a problem. Consider a complicated issue like the pros and cons of the European Union. How many people understand the issues at stake? Have you met anyone who has actually read the Maastricht Treaty? How many people could summarize (let alone deliver judgement on) an issue as complicated as the Common Agricultural Policy? Very few, I would imagine. And yet we are regularly encouraged by politicians to make up our minds 'according to the facts'. If you try to do so you may hear so many contrary opinions that you get completely swamped. Most of us, quite understandably, base many of our opinions on prejudices rather than facts. This is not because we are evil but because we simply do not have the time or the facilities to bring ourselves up to speed on the vast range of subjects that we are called upon to understand.

The trouble is that you can very quickly get into a situation where you despair of ever finding hard facts and opt for easy solutions. This plays right into the hands of those who would persuade you with attractive but flawed arguments.

There is some help to be had from playing *Reverse Know-all*, a ploy in which you concentrate on finding fault with your opponent's facts. The best way to do this is to keep pressing him to justify everything he says. Remember what grandma used to say: 'If you ask "why" often enough the world will stop turning.' It works, too! If you do not believe me just try it on yourself. There is nothing quite so destructive to an arguer's case as to have the very basis of what he says constantly brought into question.

You should practise regularly picking holes in what you hear people say on radio and television or in articles you read in the newspapers. Most people let statements go by without giving them much thought but if you develop the habit of being awkward about facts you will soon notice that quite ridiculous statements are frequently foisted upon the public with no opposition at all. Always remember Kipling's six honest serving men, What? Why? When? How? Where? and Who? Get into the habit of asking these questions constantly.

As I write, the newspapers are full of stories about people who have suffered harm by letting themselves be involved in performances by stage hypnotists. A number of cases have been quoted where people are said to have suffered dreadful consequences. One man in particular was said to have permanently regressed to the age of eight because of a hypnotic suggestion. However, there is a conspicuous lack of facts given. What man? There is no name. Who has made these claims about him? Some papers say his sister 'made a statement on behalf of the family'. The sister was not named, neither was the family. What is the medical evidence? None is given. Has he been examined by a doctor? The papers don't say. It seems unlikely that a healthy person could be permanently regressed but no psychologists, doctors or hypnotists were asked for an opinion in any of the accounts I read. Yet as I sat reading my paper on a train I overheard someone in a nearby seat telling his friend, 'It's terrible what these hypnotists can do to you. Just look at that poor chap in the papers. Doesn't bear thinking about!'

I have no idea about the true facts of that particular case but my point is that facts are what so many of the newspaper accounts conspicuously lack. If you were arguing with someone on this topic and he came out with the sort of sloppy hearsay appearing in the newspapers you would be able to tear his argument to shreds.

Always demand specific details. Always ask for the source of facts. Always question whether facts are true. These things are the armour of the successful arguer.

I once took part in a radio interview on the subject of psychometric personality testing. The interviewer was intensely hostile to the whole concept, especially when I said that one advantage of the exercise was that, since personality is not fixed like, say, your shoe size, it gave you the opportunity to iron out faults in your character. Surely, he said acidly, Freud had proved that personality was fixed in the first few years of life. Wasn't I conning gullible members of the public into believing that they could make changes that were impossible? Having read Freud I was quite sure that he had never said any such thing. In fact the whole purpose of his technique of psychoanalysis was precisely to enable patients to escape from neurotic personality disorders. My opponent was obviously making it up as he went along. So I asked him in which of Freud's writings he had come across this startling claim. He blustered a bit and, when it was quite obvious to the listeners that he did not know what he was talking about, I mischievously suggested that perhaps he had got the wrong Freud.

Maybe he had been reading Clement, the cookery writer, or Emma, the television personality, but the one he wanted was Sigmund, the psychologist.

When considering facts, whether they support your case or your opponent's, you first of all rely on the six honest serving men mentioned above. Then, equally important, you consider motivation. It is not sufficient to know where a fact comes from or what it implies; you must also understand what motivated the person who brought that fact to light.

If, for example, you read a report in the newspaper that says a recent study has revealed that sugar is not nearly as harmful to your teeth as was previously supposed, you may feel relieved. Great, let's go and eat some sweets! But wait! If you look closely you may see at the bottom of the report that, though it was written by Professors Farnsbarns and Wotsit (both leading nutrition experts) the research was paid for by the confectionery industry. Hmm! Not quite so encouraging. Many reports in the press do not give their sources sufficiently clearly and the unwary reader can come up with a misleading picture.

Also it is worth looking at the way in which information is presented. Let's take a report in two national newspapers, the *Daily Post* and the *Financial Telegraph*. The latter, an upmarket journal of impeccable reputation, reports that interest rates are about to rise by half a per cent. The *Daily Post*, a tabloid that gives little space to economics, tries to extract some drama from the situation by telling its readers: 'The Chancellor is about to hit homeowners with a whopping great half per cent rise in interest rates.' In both cases the facts are the same but the implication is entirely different.

Blinding with Science

If you have watched those advertisements on television where an actress described as a 'beauty consultant' dons a white coat and talks winningly about the wonders to be achieved by adding proteins or liposomes or neutral pH balance to some cosmetic product or other you will know immediately what is meant by *Blinding with Science*. This technique seems at first sight closely related to *Know-all* but the vital difference is that, whereas the player of *Know-all* is trying to use facts to bring some rationality into an argument, the player of *Blinding with Science* is doing just the opposite. This is where it is essential that you be well versed in the techniques of *Reverse Know-all*. The *BWS* player is very vulnerable to demands that he should justify his remarks. His strength is that he manages to sound plausible even while talking rubbish. If you are unscrupulous enough it is really quite easy to massage facts until something that is quite untrue sounds true.

Advertisers and politicians are the richest source of such arguments and it is not hard to come across a wealth of examples. These can vary from the simple to the complex. Ideally, *Blinding with Science* should involve the use of impressive sounding data, the more technical the better, combined with a manner that suggests the presenter is an acknowledged expert on his subject. Alternatively you can go for a simple, barefaced lie. For example, a well-known confectionery manufacturer relaunched one of its chocolate bars with the phrase 'Big New Size' emblazoned on the wrapper. It was smaller.

Parrot

A ploy closely related to *Know-all* relies on you spotting your opponent's mistakes and seizing on them with glee. As we saw above, few things are as destructive to an arguer's case as to be caught out in factual errors (especially if there can be a strong suggestion that the errors occurred wilfully). Therefore, having found the mistakes you take every opportunity of describing them, either to an audience or the general public, with as much scorn as you can muster. The implication must be that no one in his right mind could possibly trust a person who has such a shaky grasp of the facts of the case.

If you want to see *Parrot* played with panache you have only to watch current affairs programmes in which politicians play this game with great skill.

Naturally, if your victim is an experienced arguer he will not sit still while you mock his incompetence. He will counter-attack with allegations that you have misunderstood (either through stupidity or malice – preferably both) his whole case.

When experienced players get started on a game of *Parrot* it can last longer than Monopoly.

Nice Cop and Nasty Cop

If you have ever seen one of those movies where a tough cop and a kind cop take turns to interrogate a suspect you will know how this technique works. Although it has been overused in works of fiction it is still in frequent use in the real world and can be just as effective as it ever was.

For those who never watch police movies the technique

works like this: instead of being faced with one opponent you find yourself up against two (or more). One will be surly and aggressive, he will ask awkward questions and do his best to bully and browbeat you into submission. His partner will be Nice Cop. He will be apparently sympathetic and try to get his companion to back off and give you a chance. He will even go so far as to support your point of view on occasions. He is, in fact, playing a version of *Buddy* (q.v.).

However, Nice Cop is nowhere near as nice as he seems. He is hoping that, unable to bear the bullying of Nasty Cop, you will turn to him for support and become emotionally malleable enough to agree to whatever he proposes. The two may work simultaneously or in relays. In the latter case, after Nasty Cop has done his best to soften you up, Nice Cop will take over. He will spin you some plausible tale. He may say that Nasty Cop is a real hard bastard, that everyone hates him and that the Chief Inspector only keeps him on because he's his son-in-law. He will offer you protection from Nasty Cop but only if you will 'be reasonable'. This may mean confessing, agreeing to a lousy bargain, or in some way giving up your rights.

If you prove resistant, Nice Cop may suddenly lose patience with you and threaten to let Nasty Cop off the leash. In another scenario Nice Cop may produce a piece of surprise information known as a *Sandbag* (q.v.) and cosh you with it when you are least expecting it. Under no circumstances whatever should you trust Nice Cop. He is not only a rat but a hypocritical rat.

The best counter to this ploy is simply to expose it for what it is. If you spell out to your opponents the type of game they are playing it will make it almost impossible for them to carry on playing it. If you can also manage to make them feel foolish for having tried to catch you with such an old trick you will score twice.

Sandbag

This ploy was mentioned just a moment ago in connection with *Nice Cop and Nasty Cop* but it can be used as an adjunct to almost any other technique.

The *Sandbag* is just a catch-all term for any surprise item of information with which you can hit your opponent. The effectiveness of this ploy varies enormously, depending on what the *Sandbag* is. For example, your neighbour has complained to the authorities about loud music coming from your house and tells you so. He hopes that by letting you know you are the subject of an official complaint he can bully you into turning off the music. However, you have a friend in the council offices who has let you know on the quiet that inspectors have already been to your neighbour's house on several occasions and have been able to hear nothing untoward. Unofficially they are starting to regard your neighbour as a crank. If you can drop this nugget into the conversation the hostile neighbour will be effectively sandbagged.

Of course, you cannot always have secret information at your fingertips every time you have an argument. Even so it is surprising just how useful it is to have even quite innocuous scraps of knowledge when your opponent is unaware that you have them. If you can use these scraps to hint that your contacts are wide and your ear is firmly to the ground you will find that an opponent will treat you with much more respect.

The greatest peril with *Sandbag* is that you can make the mistake of using information that is either incorrect or out of date. Avoid this at all costs. This is the arguer's equivalent of slipping on a banana skin and your dignity will be badly dented after such a fall.

It's My Party

This is a ploy much loved by politicians but it can be used just as well by anyone engaged in a public argument. The skilful player of *It's My Party* sticks resolutely to his own agenda and treats his opponent almost as if he were superfluous to requirements. Thus, though he may offer brief answers to his opponent's questions, he will use them as a springboard to launch himself into a lengthy exposition of his own case. He will use every ounce of his strength to try to hog the conversation and prevent his opponent from either making a case himself or questioning his own case. If the opponent tries to get a word in edgeways then the player of *It's My Party* will put on an exasperated voice and growl, 'Would you please let me finish what I am saying!', for all the world as though he were the injured party. Self-righteousness is the very essence of a skilled player's game.

It's My Party is not really suitable as a tactic for private arguments because these usually have a flexible time limit and both players may carry on battling until they feel they have had their say. However, as we saw earlier, one of the defining characteristics of a public argument is that it has a time limit. It is therefore greatly to the advantage of the player who can take up most of that time by putting his own case. Remember also that in a public argument the players are not really trying to convince each other but are far more concerned with their audience. A good game of *It's My Party* will impress the audience with the merits of the player's case while preventing adversaries from asking too many awkward questions.

Almost all politicians will repay close observation if you want to learn how this ploy is best used. Mrs Thatcher may be remembered as one of the really great players of modern times but even she paled into insignificance when compared to Harold Macmillan. In the post-war years, when home-building was very high on the political agenda, Macmillan used to give the impression that he never thought of anything else. Any question put to him by the Press, no matter on what subject, would provoke a remark about the excellence of the government's house-building record. The strange thing about *It's My Party* is that, although at the time it is perfectly obvious that the player is indulging in a devious ploy, ultimately it still works to his advantage.

Friend of the Boss

This describes the practice of going over someone's head when you feel that you are not getting the required results. You might question whether, strictly speaking, this constitutes winning an argument. In many circumstances it smacks of running away from one. However, this book is concerned with getting results and *Friend of the Boss*, when played skilfully, will achieve that. Of course, you do not actually have to be a friend of the boss to play this game (though it would help). All you have to do is go to the superior of whoever is causing you problems and complain. Ideally you should have a legitimate complaint. In fact, if the person with whom the argument started is being deliberately obstructive there is every reason why you should go over his head. However, there are many occasions when people (especially those who regard themselves as being in some way socially superior) use the technique to get those further down the ladder into a spot of bother. The success or otherwise of the technique depends as much as anything on the attitude of the boss in question. If he is the sort of person who sticks by his staff through thick and thin you may get a dusty answer. However, many bosses find it distressingly easy to believe that their staff are lazy, rude and incompetent and will regard any complaint as proved the moment it is made.

If you really want to use this ploy to its best advantage you should combine it with *Buddy* (q.v.). You approach the boss with the attitude that you, being an important and busy person, understand only too well his problems. Naturally you do not think for one moment that he is responsible for the disgusting treatment you have received at the hands of his underlings. Indeed you are doing him a favour by enlightening him on this point and giving him the chance he craves to save the reputation of his business. This may sound creepy and disingenuous. It is. And it works.

Bulldozer

This is the most aggressive of all offensive tactics and the very fact that you are reading this book means you are probably not suited to playing *Bulldozer*. It is simply an attempt to bludgeon your way to victory by sheer force of personality. It is a tactic used by forceful, dominant and, usually, successful people. The journalist Bryan Appleyard gave a good description of *Bulldozer* when writing about the former editor of the *Sunday Times*, Andrew Neil:

> Neil always carries a gun to a knife fight, seldom loses in debate and is never stuck for words. His conference style is devastating and his broadcasting persona radiates a disori-

entating charm so that, even when he is being flagrantly wrong-headed, he can appear to be right through sheer force of his presence. And that, on television, is usually all that matters.

If you are capable of playing *Bulldozer* effectively then throw this book away or give it to some less forceful soul who needs it. If you are not, then is there anything you can do against it? To be quite honest, probably not much. You may be able to score some useful debating points by using *Know-all*. You may even be able to *Sandbag* your opponent. However, the people who play *Bulldozer* are usually professional arguers and, though you may take the odd game off them you are unlikely to win a whole set. Even when they compete against each other it is unusual to see anyone knocked out. If you watch politicians doing battle with television interviewers you will notice that, even though the politician may be completely and utterly in the wrong, he will never be stuck for words and will still be able to make a forceful and plausible sounding case no matter how misguided. The only advice to give in these circumstance is, don't play out of your league.

Mad Dog

People who play *Bulldozer* are usually intelligent and articulate even though they relish aggression. *Mad Dog* is a close relative of Bulldozer but it requires very little skill. In plain English, *Mad Dog* is just old-fashioned bullying. People who play this game turn red in the face, thump the table and shout. If you try to argue back they just shout even louder and hope that you will be intimidated. This is crass behaviour but, as with other forms of bullying, it works often enough to make it attractive to a certain type of person. Trying to respond to a *Mad Dog* player with a display of temperament of your own is not a good idea. You will either end up taking part in an unproductive shouting match or you will get involved in a fight. Neither of these is a good way to win.

The only effective way to counter a *Mad Dog* player is to weather the storm and then destroy him with the other tactics you have learned. Remember that even a hurricane must blow itself out and even the most impassioned *Mad Dog* player can be brought under control, though it may not be easy.

People who bully are usually weak on facts and have poor stamina. A counter-attack that uses *Know-all* and is backed up by the *Chinese Water Torture* will often be very effective. Although it is hard to do, keeping calm in the face of aggression can be extremely irritating to the aggressor. It can actually hurt him far more than a punch in the teeth, especially if you have an audience, because it makes him look cheap and shallow.

Hearsay

Here we have a very effective but thoroughly dishonest technique which you may choose to use yourself but which, at all costs, you must recognize when it is used against you.

There is an honourable version of *Hearsay* that is used by journalists. They will often preface a question with a phrase such as: 'Some people may say that . . . ' or 'But what of people who object that . . . '. This is a perfectly fair way of seeking to put an alternative view. The journalist may not be representing his own opinions but is acting as devil's advocate or representing the public by putting contrary views and asking the interviewee to defend his position.

However, there is a much sleazier version in which your opponent hides behind what other people, usually anonymous, have said about you.

'I don't believe it myself, but people are saying that you beat your wife. Of course, no one really thinks for a moment that it's true but some people say they saw you hit her on several occasions. Isn't it terrible the way people gossip?'

The trouble with *Hearsay* is that it is impossible to defend yourself against it. The more you protest against what has been said the more your persecutor will insist that he agrees with you. Then he will carry on repeating even more scurrilous allegations happily aware that you can do nothing to defend yourself.

You can, of course, maintain that things said by anonymous people are worthless and that if anyone has anything to say about you he should say it to your face. However, it is hard to stop attacks of this sort. Your opponent will insist ever more urgently that he is truly on your side and that he agrees with everything you say. This is a cowardly tactic that belongs in the dirty tricks department but, because it is so often effective, it is unlikely to fall into disuse.

Reverse Psychology

Most people have heard of reverse psychology but, in case you have not, it involves using the natural cussedness of human nature to persuade someone to do what you want by appearing to argue for the opposite. Confused?

I used to have trouble getting my young son to come

upstairs for his bath. No matter how I wheedled and cajoled he would run away, hide and scream if I tried to force him. So then I simply forbade him to come upstairs: 'Alexander, stay down there!' I yelled. 'Can't you see how busy I am? I just don't have time to play with you in the bath. No, I'm sorry, I just can't. Daddy has a lot of work to do.' In the end I would, reluctantly, relent and allow him, as a special treat and on this occasion only, to get into the bath. It's surprising how well this worked. Even when he was a little older and wiser in the wicked ways of parents it was very difficult for him to resist the temptation of an absolute prohibition.

If you think that adults are too sophisticated for this sort of trickery then you are in for a surprise. It works just as well on people who think themselves clever. However, to make it work you must be a good and convincing actor. Being plain sneaky also helps. For example, instead of you being the one to propose the course of action you do not want your opponent to follow, try getting someone else who is genuinely opposed to do it for you. For example, have you ever noticed how when some sexually explicit or violent movie receives publicity there is no shortage of people to take a high moral tone and condemn it roundly? And what happens? Everyone rushes to see it, of course. One could be forgiven for suspecting that the moral outrage is often encouraged, and maybe even instigated, by the publicists working for the movie company.

Of course, the danger with *Reverse Psychology* is that you may misjudge your opponent and end up convincing him of the merits of your case. Into every life a little rain must fall.

Clown

Clown was first introduced to me by a French-Canadian friend when I was very young and had just started in my first job. My boss was a dry old stick who had never had children, did not understand young people, and did not like the fact that I had a university degree and he hadn't. We did not get on. However, he was the boss and he had the ability to make my life extremely uncomfortable, which he proceeded to do in a number of ingenious ways.

One evening I was telling my friend about the problem. 'You're afraid of him, aren't you?' she asked. Funnily enough I had not considered this possibility. I had assumed that I hated and despised him but, on consideration, I had to admit that he frightened me.

'This is what you do,' she said. 'Every time he calls you in to see him you must imagine that he is sitting on the loo suffering from a dreadful attack of diarrhoea. You'll be amazed how it works. Once you convince yourself that he is ridiculous you will never be frightened of him again. And as soon as you stop being frightened and stand up to him he will back off.'

So I tried it and it worked. I cannot claim that overnight the boss became putty in my hands. However, I did pluck up enough courage to challenge him to his face. I pointed out to him that his dislike of me was personal and had nothing to do with any faults in my work. He blustered a bit and issued some routine denials but from that time on he backed off and left me alone.

Since then I have used *Clown* on many occasions, though nowadays I find Monique's version a little Freudian for my taste. The principle still holds good: anything you can do to make your opponent seem ridiculous will strengthen your position. If you are engaged in a public argument and can belittle your opponent in front of the onlookers so much the better.

One variation of *Clown* that anyone can use is called *Marcel Marceau* after the French mime artist. When engaged in an argument on the telephone you can mime your dislike of your opponent. Make rude faces and gestures to your heart's content; he can't see you. Gestures that you may consider too forceful or too rude to use in a face-to-face confrontation can be very effectively used on the phone. You should allow yourself complete freedom to express exactly how you feel. Stick your tongue out, give him the finger, be as childish as you like. You will find that the silent display of contempt allows you to keep your temper in the most trying conditions.

Another form of *Clown* is called *Fly Swat* and is best used in public arguments where you have an audience. *Fly Swat* is simply the technique much used by stand-up comedians for putting down hecklers. If you are one of those lucky people who have a ready wit and a sharp tongue you will always be able to think up a suitably cutting remark to bring your opponent down a peg or two. If you find that sort of thing difficult then you should take a tip from the comedians and have a little repertoire of crushing remarks you can trot out at will. But take care, you must regularly replenish your stock so that they always sound fresh. A tired old line you have been heard to use before (or that has been used on television so often that everybody knows it) will not do much for your reputation.

It is also vital to ensure that your put-down is delivered appropriately. For example, an elderly woman comes into your office to make a complaint but is far ruder than the complaint justifies. Do you turn to your audience, smile sardonically and quip, 'Three million sperm and this one had to get through.' No, it sounds vulgar and offensive. However, if you used the same line on the drunk in the pub who insists on rubbishing your favourite football team you would get a laugh and win a reputation for wit (of sorts).

Hand Grenade

My father often told me a story about a commanding officer he had during the Second World War. On one occasion this man finished his meal in the officers' mess, stood up, pulled a live Mill's grenade from his pocket, removed the pin, deposited the grenade on the dining table and left the room. The effect on his fellow officers was dramatic.

I would not go as far as to advise you to copy this behaviour but you can learn from it the advantages of surprise. Anything you can do to disconcert an opponent will help to make winning the argument easier.

George Melly the jazz singer once wrote about an occasion when he was menaced by Teddy boys (yes, this is an old story) outside a jazz club where he had been appearing. They had him pretty well cornered and were snarling around trying to provoke him into doing something that would give them the excuse to hit him. Obviously aggression was out of the question – there were too many of them. Pleading was also out – there is no surer way of getting hit than to show you are afraid. In the end he took from his pocket a slim volume of poetry and read them a tone poem. Though I remember the story well the words of the poem escape me. This is because they went something like: 'Bop bedop ba ba di doo daah.' (I apologize to the poet for this crass misquotation.) However, the ploy worked extremely well. There simply is no suitable response to someone who responds to threats of violence with an avant-garde poem. The Teddy boys muttered obscene threats but the cue for physical violence had simply not been given and in the end they shuffled off to find another victim.

Another example of *Hand Grenade* (and I swear this is a true story) is of a young man who went for a job interview and found that he was one of a couple of dozen applicants. The potential employer, an American, had asked an English company with which he did business to see all the applicants and narrow them down to a reasonable number. He would then fly over from the States, interview the short-listed candidates, and choose a winner.

How was he going to be remembered among all that throng? The young man went to the toilet, took off his waistcoat and put it on again over the top of his suit. He then went into the interview, took off his overcoat, hung it on the coat rack and, ignoring the puzzled looks of his inquisitor, answered all the questions with aplomb. At no stage did he seek to explain his odd appearance. It worked. The interviewer was intrigued, puzzled and amused, and could not wait to tell his American friend the story. The young man was duly invited to join the short list.

Thin End of the Wedge

This technique is familiar to most of us but is well worth adding to your arsenal of argument-winning ploys. It relies for its effectiveness on wringing a small concession from your opponent and then using that weakening of his position to get progressively larger concessions.

Like all the techniques discussed here, this one is double-edged and requires caution. To settle an argument it is usually necessary to make concessions of some sort.

Shooting the Fox

There are two main ways of dealing with foxes. Ladies and gentlemen dress up smartly, mount fine horses, and have a splendid time chasing them all over the countryside before finally watching them being torn to bits by hounds. Farmers shoot them. It is considered unsporting but is quick and effective.

For our present purposes to shoot a fox is to bring an argument to a sudden conclusion by cutting through the peripherals and getting to the heart of the matter in one stroke.

Often people get to love an argument for its own sake. Indeed they can get so wrapped up in it that they lose sight of its original purpose. If you have the wit and presence of mind to grasp what is essential you can score a speedy and decisive victory.

Take as an example the controversy surrounding the Shroud of Turin. This holy relic was traditionally supposed to be the shroud that had covered the body of Christ. In some miraculous way the image of Jesus' body had become printed on the cloth and could, using a photographic negative, be clearly seen. But was it genuine?

It was a truly fascinating argument with endless ramifications. For example, the image was only clearly visible, as mentioned before, if you first photographed the cloth and then viewed the photographic negative. Yet, even if the shroud was, as some suspected, a fake, it certainly predated the invention of photography by many years. How could anyone produce a fake that was only visible using a process that had not yet been invented?

The complications were endless. The nail holes in the body were in the correct place. Traditionally painters and sculptors had shown Christ's wounds to be in his hands. Anatomically and historically this was nonsense because the hands would not have borne such a weight. The actual method of crucifixion was to drive the nails through the wrist bones. The shroud showed this quite accurately. On the other hand the image on the shroud showed the hands modestly covering the genitals, but if a body has been 'laid out' the hands would not normally reach so far. Also the image showed that blood had run from the wounds. Biblical evidence tells us that the body was washed before burial and, of course, dead bodies do not bleed.

This argument looked set to go on for ever. It got extremely heated and some of the scholars involved got so emotionally and intellectually bound up in the struggle that religious conversions were reported to have taken place among them.

Then, at long last, permission was given to take a small portion of the shroud and subject it to carbon dating. The results were conclusive. The cloth was of such late manufacture that the image could not be genuine. The fox had been shot.

In a way it was a pity that such an entertaining argument should come to such an abrupt end. Many of the issues that had been raised were interesting and worthy of serious consideration but, once the fox was dead, they were quickly disregarded by all but a dedicated few.

Defensive Tactics

What of defence? There is a whole range of things you can do to help defuse an argument. Some of these techniques are constructive and some are not. Let's look at the constructive ones first.

Logician

Logic is an integral part of any argument. However, it is surprising how often people seek to disguise nonsense by making it appear to be logical. This is not the place to discuss logic at length (there are plenty of books that will give you an introduction to that arcane branch of philosophy), but it will be useful to see the ways in which logic can be used to trick you.

A relative of mine, a vicar, regularly used to trot out the following argument in favour of the validity of the Christian religion. If the truths of Christianity were actually false then Christ had died in vain, all the saints and martyrs had been in error, all the clerics in the history of the world had been wrong and all the prayers of the countless faithful had gone for nothing. Could such a catastrophe really have occurred? Of course not! It was simply unthinkable that such a vast edifice could ever crumble.

This argument used to fascinate me. It was delivered with great sincerity by a man who was by no means stupid and yet he never noticed a gaping flaw in his logic. Nor, as far as I am aware, did any of his parishioners ever spot the mistake. For if his argument was true in relation to Christianity it was also true in relation to every other major religion. However, since the major religions mostly claim to be uniquely true and exclude each other then the argument must of necessity be false in relation to some of them.

This is a fine example of false logic. Logicians recognize numerous fallacies. Here is a list based on one compiled long ago by Irving M. Copi of the University of Michigan for use by his students. It contains all the fallacies you should look out for in your opponents' arguments and avoid in your own.

1 Argumentum ad Baculum (appeal to force)

This fallacy occurs when one appeals to force or the threat of force to cause acceptance of a conclusion. A famous example occurred when Churchill mentioned an opinion of the Pope's to Stalin at the Yalta Conference. Stalin is supposed to have replied, 'And how many divisions has the Pope?'

2 Argumentum ad Hominem (abusive)

This translates as 'argument directed towards the man'. The abusive variety occurs when an argument is dismissed on the basis that the person proposing that view is unworthy of respect. Thus to argue that someone's view is flawed because he is a Catholic or a Communist or a Fascist, or whatever, is fallacious. The argument must be allowed to stand or fall by itself and not because of our opinion of its proponent.

3 Argumentum ad Hominem (circumstantial)

If two people are arguing and one ignores the question of

whether his own contention is true and tries to persuade his opponent to accept it because of his special circumstances, then that is the circumstantial *Argumentum ad Hominem*. An example would be where two people are arguing over the morality of fox hunting. One insists that watching an animal being torn to pieces for fun is barbaric. The other replies, 'But you're a butcher, so what right have you to disagree?' The argument has been falsely focused upon one of the arguers rather than on the issue at stake.

4 Argumentum ad Ignoratium (argument from ignorance)

If one argues that a proposition is true simply because it has never been proved false, that is the argument from ignorance. An example would be to argue that there must be ghosts because no one has ever proved that there aren't any.

5 Argumentum ad Misericordiam (appeal to pity)

The appeal to pity arises when one party to an argument seeks to gain the advantage by throwing aside questions of reason and tries instead to invoke the sympathy of his listeners. The ludicrous example usually given as an illustration is the case of a young man accused of the particularly horrible murder of his parents. He pleaded for leniency on the grounds that he was an orphan.

6 Argumentum ad Populum

In this fallacy an emotional appeal is used to whip up popular opinion to support an argument without reference to its logical worth. It is the favourite trick of demagogues and rabble-rousers the world over. If you want a more elegant example you should recall Mark Antony's funeral oration over the body of Caesar in Shakespeare's *Julius Caesar*.

7 Argumentum ad Verecundiam (appeal to authority)

An appeal to the opinions of a great or famous person only supports an argument if that person was peculiarly qualified in the relevant field. For example, if you appeal to the opinion of Einstein on a question of relativity you will be on safe ground, but if your argument is about cricket then the appeal would be in vain. This may sound obvious but it is quite common to cite famous people in this way. It is also far from unusual for such people to put themselves forward as experts simply on the grounds that they are well known and respected by the public.

8 Accident

The accidental fallacy consists in applying a general rule to a particular case whose accidental circumstances render the rule inapplicable. (In this context, 'accidental' means 'nonessential' or 'incidental', rather than 'by chance'.) Students of logic are sometimes given this jokey example to help them remember: 'What you bought yesterday, you eat today. You bought raw meat yesterday, therefore you eat raw meat today.'

9 Converse Accident (hasty generalization)

If we try to generalize from observing all cases of a certain kind we find that we can usually only pay attention to some of them. If those examined are atypical rather than typical then the conclusion drawn may well be a converse accident. Thus if we look at cases of people struck by lightning but only focus on those where the victim survived we might build up an impressive case for believing that lightning is not very dangerous after all.

10 False Cause

This covers any argument that falsely assumes a causal connection between two events. For example, it used to be believed in some cultures that beating drums and letting off fireworks would stop an eclipse by scaring off the monster that was trying to eat the sun. Of course, thanks to the infrequency of solar eclipses, it appeared to work, and thus the false cause was regularly reinforced. It is easy to laugh at the supposed simplicity of people in earlier ages but false cause is still at the root of many invalid arguments. Not long ago Great Britain had a run of hot, dry summers accompanied in many parts by a severe drought. Many people put this down to the onset of global warming, a phenomenon that was receiving a lot of media attention. For a while many people were quite convinced that the earth's atmosphere was indeed getting noticeably and significantly hotter. Then there was a run of the sort of cool, wet summers the British are used to and the enthusiasm for this particular explanation declined.

11 Denying the Antecedent

In a conditional statement of the form, 'If ... then ... ', the first part, after the 'if' and before the 'then', is called the antecedent. The part after the 'then' is called the consequent. Denying the antecedent refers to the fallacy of inferring that the consequent of a conditional statement is false, given that the conditional statement is true and the antecedent is false. Here is an example. 'If there are engineering works at Clapham Junction then the 5.45 train will be late.' 'If there are no engineering works at Clapham Junction then the 5.45 train will not be late.' The first conditional statement may be true, but the second does not follow from it.

12 Petitio Principii (begging the question)

This assumes a premise that cannot be known to be true unless the conclusion is true. What happens is that the premise and the conclusion are the same but formulated differently. This makes it look to the casual observer as if something profound has been said when the argument is in fact quite empty. Irving Copi used to quote the following example:

> 'To allow every man unbounded freedom of speech must always be, on the whole, advantageous to the state; for it is highly conducive to the interests of the community that each individual should enjoy a liberty, perfectly unlimited, of expressing his sentiments.'

13 Complex Question

Complex questions are questions that contain assumptions or damaging assertions that have not been proved to be true. The most famous example is, 'When did you stop beating your wife?' But there are many others, such as, 'What did you do with the stolen goods?', or 'Why is the privatization of industry so much more efficient than state control?'. No matter how they are answered, the damaging assertions contained in these questions tend to incriminate the respondent.

14 Simple Conversion

This is the form of fallacious inference by which one proposition is obtained as the converse of another proposition. If you say 'All A is B' you are not logically entitled to conclude 'All B is A'. For example, 'All thieves are criminals' may be true but you cannot reverse the proposition and say that 'All criminals are thieves.' You can, of course, say 'No A is B, therefore no B is A.' Thus, 'No thief is a law-abiding citizen, therefore no law-abiding citizen is a thief.'

15 Undistributed Middle

In a syllogism, which is a deductive inference consisting of two premises and a conclusion, the 'middle' is the term that occurs in both premises but not the conclusion. If the middle is 'undistributed' – i.e. if we only know about some members of the class designated by the term – then the conclusion is fallacious. For example, 'All thieves are criminals, some criminals are insane, therefore some thieves are insane,' is fallacious because the middle term 'criminals' is undistributed, i.e. we are only told about some of them, not all of them. It would be OK to say, however, 'Some men are thieves, all thieves are criminals, therefore some men are criminals', because in this case the middle term 'thieves' *is* distributed – we *are* told about all of them.

16 Ignoratio Elenchi (irrelevant conclusion)

This fallacy consists of producing a proof that validly proves something but not the thing it was required to prove. For example, if a politician is arguing for the return of the death penalty on the grounds that it is a deterrent, and supplies evidence to show that violent crime has risen in Great Britain since the last person was hanged in 1964, then, however valid that evidence might be in proving that violent crime had risen, it does *not* prove that the death penalty is a deterrent. That would be drawing an irrelevant conclusion.

17 Equivocation

Sometimes this term is loosely used as a synonym for any form of dishonest argument, particularly that which relies on verbal sleight of hand. However, in logic, equivocation is what is termed a 'fallacy of ambiguity'. In our language there are many words that have more than one meaning, such as post, ground and play. Normally the context in which such words are used ensures that no misunderstanding takes place and, unless we are making an intentional pun, we hardly notice the oddity of such words. However, what happens if a word is used in more than one sense in the same argument? The example usually quoted is: 'The end of a thing is its perfection; death is the end of life; hence death is the perfection of life.' The ambiguity is introduced by using the word 'end' firstly in the sense of 'goal' and secondly in the sense of 'last event'. Both meanings are legitimate but, by confusing them, the writer has produced a logical fallacy.

Another fallacy of ambiguity arises when 'relative' words are used. For example, the expressions 'a tall man' and 'a tall tree' contain quite different concepts of height even though the word 'tall' is used each time. Again, most of the time, we have no problem. However, take a word like 'good'. If you say, 'Fred Brown is a good man, he had a good record in the last war and now he will make a good Prime Minister,' you will be using the word 'good' ambiguously to create a fallacious argument.

Stonewall

Do you really need to argue at all? For many people the mere fact that someone else opposes their point of view is sufficient to tempt them into an argument. This may not be a wise move. In some circumstances simply refusing to be drawn into conflict can be an extremely powerful weapon. Assuming that you are sufficiently confident of your position, why should you bother giving your would-be opponent the satisfaction of being taken seriously? As an example, let's take two neighbours who fall out over the building of an extension. Mr Brown says the building will be an eyesore, will block his light, invade his privacy and devalue his property. Mr Jones, however, knows he can go ahead. He has planning permission and he is breaking no laws. Some people might still feel that they had to argue their case with Brown and try to justify their position. But why? What will it achieve? Sometimes the most effective tactic is to do absolutely nothing.

Breaker

The object of *Breaker* is to try to split the argument up into its component parts to see if there are any areas of agreement between the parties. Using this technique demonstrates a certain amount of goodwill on your part and encourages your opponent to reciprocate. *Breaker* is a prelude to negotiation.

What tends to happen in many arguments is that the parties become so emotionally involved that they lose sight of their true objectives. Let's take an example: a neighbour erects a high fence at the side of your property. Even though the fence is not large enough to require planning permission you feel that it blocks your view and that erecting it was a deliberately unfriendly act on the part of your neighbour. Very quickly the argument progresses beyond the issue of the fence. The fact that it was erected at all shows that your neighbour never liked you and is physical proof that he rejects you. Very soon you start to go over in your mind all the slights, real or imagined, you have ever had to suffer from this man. Then the other neighbours start to get drawn in. People you talk to remind you that he parks his car inconsiderately in the street and neglects his front garden which has become an eyesore.

By now the neighbour has realized that you have been talking about him and a row develops. He confronts you and, to your surprise and annoyance, produces a similar list of complaints about your behaviour.

You see how, by this stage, the argument has become diffuse and irrational. People are angry, resentful and over-emotional.

It is at this point that *Breaker* can be used effectively. If you can sit down with your opponent and go through all the issues that divide you it may be possible to settle at least some of them. Perhaps you could persuade him to park his car differently and mow his lawn occasionally. You might be able to make some concessions yourself. By the time you get back to the key issue of the fence you should, with luck, have established an atmosphere of cooperation rather than confrontation. Once you are both in a state of mind to compromise it may appear that the issue of the fence is less intractable than you thought. Maybe your neighbour was acting from the best of motives and only trying to provide a bit of privacy for both of you.

The trouble with *Breaker*, as with all constructive moves, is that it requires maturity, tact and diplomacy. It might not come as naturally as bickering, bullying, beefing or bitching, nor will it satisfy your lust for an out-and-out battle. The trouble with argument is that it appeals strongly to the child within us and rejects the sensible advice of the parent who also lurks inside. However, it is vital that the parent should win because the frustrated child's solutions are invariably violent and destructive.

If you cannot play *Breaker* yourself because the emotional charge that has been allowed to build up is too great, then maybe you should find a third party to act as mediator. This could be a neutral neighbour, a mutual friend, or even a professional mediator.

However you do it you must find a way to break out of the grip of this sort of argument.

Buddy

On the surface *Buddy* may appear to be a defensive tactic but it may well have offensive undertones. The ploy is to try to get round an opponent by appealing to him as a human being and trying to enlist his sympathy. This works best when your opponent represents some organization, the larger and more impersonal the better. You will take the line that, of course, we are reasonable people who need not be sucked into all this stupidity. You may adopt whatever enthusiasms your opponent exhibits: if he seems keen on children, then so are you; if you discover that he's a football fanatic, then you are intensely interested in finding out who he fancies for the cup.

Once a rapport has been established you can easily use it to try to persuade your new friend to overlook corporate interests in the name of friendship. If you have played your hand properly, you will not even have to ask.

Buddy is not the easiest ploy to use. Of course, if you are one of those naturally charming types who genuinely likes people and is able to get on with all sorts, then this technique will suit you well. But, of course, if you are that sort of person then you will not need me to tell you how to exploit your talent, you will have been doing it very successfully since infancy. For the rest of us, employing *Buddy* requires effort and the application of whatever acting skills we possess. This can be dangerous because there are few things more off-putting than a false show of friendship and people are usually very quick to recognize when someone is trying to use them.

It will have occurred to you by now that this technique is rather manipulative. However, as I said at the beginning, you don't have to use these techniques but you do have to be aware of them in case they are used on you.

Buddy is, of course, the antithesis of *Wimp-out* techniques such as *I Only Work Here* (q.v.). You may well find that an opponent who does not want to play with you will employ a *Wimp-out* technique to spoil your ploy. His line will be, 'I'd love to be your Buddy, but They won't let me.'

Wimp-out

This is not one technique; it is a whole family of them. *Wimp-out* covers all those tactics in which you pretend to be in the grip of forces greater than yourself. The most common gambit of this type is *Don't Blame Me I Only Work Here.* Nobody who has ever been at the mercy of petty officialdom can fail to recognize this tactic. It depends on the perpetrator presenting himself as a mere pawn in the power of his employer or some other higher power. No matter what you say or do he will steadfastly insist that it is not he who is the cause of your trouble and, of course, if he had his way he would immediately do as you ask. However, *I Only Work Here* so nothing can be done.

First cousin to this technique is the *Evil Master*. In this gambit the player insists that, though he himself is a decent, honest and reasonable chap, his boss is the sort of evil swine who eats small children and mugs old ladies for fun. The *Evil Master* need not be a single individual, it could be the Board, the Council, the Government, or any other body that can conveniently lift responsibility from the individual. Play proceeds along the same lines as *I Only Work Here*. The object of the game is a complete abnegation of responsibility in the face of hostile argument.

One way of dealing with players of *Evil Master* is to insist on meeting the creature face to face. Asking for a meeting with the person in charge may have the desired effect but, on the other hand, some organizations are so constructed that it seems no one is actually in charge. Many years ago I worked for the Civil Service as a research assistant. When I had been there a while it occurred to me that all my colleagues also had titles that included the word 'assistant' or 'deputy'. Nobody in the entire place seemed to have the authority to do anything; they merely helped some anonymous higher being to do it. This whole system was pernicious because it led to a state of mind in which no one ever accepted responsibility.

The chief disadvantage of playing any form of *Wimp-out* is that it quickly destroys the respect that anyone may have for you. By appearing to be always at the mercy of higher powers you will inevitably make yourself look weedy to your opponent who will very soon cease to take you seriously in any capacity.

Wimp-out may be allowed to become a bad mental habit (the psychological equivalent of biting your nails) and, if that happens, you risk losing your self-respect. If you develop a habit of always referring decisions upwards you will soon find yourself incapable of decision. We have all come across petty bureaucrats to whom this has happened and they are not a pretty sight.

Are there any circumstances in which *Wimp-out* is a good tactic? The only one I can think of is when it is used dishonestly. You may use the *Evil Master* as a backstop to prevent you being forced into making concessions. When the heat of argument becomes too great to bear you can always claim that you need to refer back to your boss for a decision, even when this is not strictly true. If this is used only as an occasional emergency technique then it can be a useful way to get yourself out of a tight spot. But the warning given above still applies – don't let yourself look weedy.

Lightning Conductor

Sally, who used to be my assistant many years ago, taught me the use of this technique. Sally was a good worker, a bright girl who should have succeeded in her career. Unfortunately she was also a girl with a complicated family history; she carried a great load of anger around with her. I soon discovered that Sally would let the anger build up inside her and then would have to release it explosively at the nearest available person. Sometimes the person was me.

Lightning Conductor worked like this: I would pick subjects on whom Sally could vent her anger. Since she was easily moved to rage it was never difficult. At one time she would hate someone in Accounts; another time someone in the

Design department would incur her wrath. These animosities were rather tame affairs for the most part and consisted almost entirely of bitching about the victims behind their backs. All I had to do was nod sympathetically and agree that Helen, Robin, Susan or whoever was indeed the most unpleasant, sneaky or snobbish person I had ever met.

This worked extremely well. As long as Sally was kept supplied with hate figures she remained an affable person whose work was beyond reproach. However, these animosities, based as they were on little real substance, had a habit of burning themselves out. If I failed to notice in time that the fire was dying for lack of fuel I would be in great danger of becoming a victim myself. Sally would start giving me sidelong glances and passing acid little remarks that were designed to provoke a quarrel. If I did not recognize these early warning signs for what they were I would soon find myself under attack.

So much for Sally and her problems. How does this help you to argue better? Well, the principle of the *Lightning Conductor* can be applied to many situations. If you can supply your opponent with a hate object that serves his purpose better than you do, then you may well be able to deflect his attentions.

This technique needs to be used with great care. In Sally's case I knew that no matter how much she fulminated against her enemies she would never do anything to hurt them. Not everyone is as harmless as Sally. Many people will happily employ scapegoats to take the heat off themselves.

At its worst this technique can lead to the most vicious sort of persecution. Recent history is littered with stories of minority groups that have been hounded, harassed and murdered because some rabble-rouser decided that they would make a good *Lightning Conductor*. I said at the beginning of this chapter that some of the techniques would be of questionable morality and this is a particularly good example. However, you should be aware of all the techniques that are available.

Lightning Conductor can be used as an adjunct to *Buddy*. In this case you try to get your opponent on your side by offering him some third party whom you can both hate. It could be anyone at all: a mutual acquaintance, the government, the boss, the Company. It really is of no importance who becomes the scapegoat: the important consideration is that your opponent should hate the scapegoat more than he hates you. In fact he should hate him so much that, in comparison, you appear to be almost a friend.

Although this technique is dangerous and can have tragic results I have seen it work to great benefit. I once worked in an office where everyone, but everyone, hated the same person. The man in question had almost elected himself to the position. He was fanatically hard working, always saw every question from the company's point of view, was given to sarcasm and faultfinding, spent his few idle moments checking up on his colleagues and reporting them to the boss – in short, he was a creep. It was, however, the happiest office I have ever worked in. Everyone spent so much time hating this one individual that they got on with each other splendidly.

The Wellington Boot

Here we have a sneaky, but essentially harmless, tactic that you can practise with a reasonably clear conscience.

There was once a portrait painter with something of a reputation among the rich and famous. However, though he was gratified to get so much business he did find his clients awfully pernickety and he resented their crass and ill-informed comments on his work. Then he came up with an idea. In each portrait he would include, somewhere in the background, a Wellington boot. Eventually the patron would see the picture and, sure as fate, would seize upon the boot and ask what the devil it was doing there. The artist would then fight a splendid battle in which he insisted that the boot was a vital part of the composition. Without it the whole ambience would be absolutely ruined. Sometimes he won his point and sometimes he lost. It hardly mattered which. What really mattered was that the patron was so busy arguing over the wretched boot that he neglected to criticize the rest of the painting.

That story may be apocryphal but I have seen the *Wellington Boot* in action and it does work. One publishing company I worked in had a boss whose intellectual gifts were quite frighteningly acute. Unfortunately he knew it and made quite sure that everyone else knew it too. When work was presented to him for inspection he would inevitably start to pick it to pieces. Of course, this did much to reduce the amount of sloppy work in the company and, to that extent, it was a good thing. The trouble was that no matter how hard you prepared and what lengths you went to to get everything perfect, Kenneth would find fault. He could not help it, he was just built that way. Eventually people started to use the *Wellington Boot*. They would include a deliberate error so glaring that it brought the wrath of God down straight away. This was bad, but it was over quickly and the chances were that having discovered one really good mistake he would not bother looking for others.

Wellington Boots come in all shapes and sizes. Any unlikely distraction will serve to get your opponent away from areas you would rather avoid. Persistently wandering off the topic under discussion, for example, can provide a wonderful distraction. It will not help you win an argument but it will keep you from losing one. Albert, an old friend whose job includes keeping a large committee in order, used to say, 'I could tell they weren't in a mood to agree to my proposal so I started talking rubbish about something else. By next time we meet they'll have forgotten all about it and I'll be able to get it past them.'

China Egg

If you have ever kept chickens you will know that a china egg will sometimes encourage them to lay real eggs. The application of this technique to humans was described by Hugh (later Lord) Cudlipp, the one-time chairman of the *Daily Mirror*. He was fond of telling how he would take a promising young writer out to lunch and, during the course of conversation, would skilfully place a china egg in the form of a good idea for a newspaper article. The writer would enthusiastically seize upon the idea and proceed to develop it in the course of conversation. Quite soon he would be convinced that the idea was his own and, having had his confidence greatly boosted, would go on to produce further ideas.

The technique as applied to arguments is subtly different. Here you seek to avoid an open argument by very carefully getting your opponent to accept your ideas as his own. This has to be done with great skill. In many cases it is best to use this technique in combination with a bit of *Reverse Psychology*. The way to do this is to start by outlining the position you wish your opponent to reject. Preferably you should put the words into the mouth of some third party of whom you are sure your opponent will disapprove. As soon as you see that the victim has seized the bait you go on to encourage him to come up with the solution that you have already chosen. It is vital that at all times he regards this solution as his own. When he produces it you congratulate him warmly on his perspicacity and, if you have brass neck enough, even thank him profusely for having cleared this issue up for you.

Elsewhere in this book I have said that I doubt that there are distinct differences between men's and women's styles of argument. However, if I were forced to choose one technique that is strongly female in character, *China Egg* would be it. Just as children have a natural talent for *Chinese Water Torture*, so women excel at *China Egg*. I have frequently overheard my wife's friends saying, 'I always let him think he thought of it first . . . ' when describing how they conned their husband into making a decision. Sometimes I wonder just how many of my own good ideas have been planted in the same way.

Other Men's Shoes

This technique comes with a health warning attached. It is powerful, it works, but it is a two-edged sword. Handle with extreme caution! American Indians are said to have a proverb, 'Never criticize a man until you have walked all day in his moccasins.' This sounds like one of those bits of apocryphal wisdom, but it works. You can gather a great deal of useful insights into an opponent's strategy if you look at matters from his point of view. You can work out the sort of arguments he might use, you can gather facts that would be disadvantageous to your own case, you can imagine why your opponent feels so aggrieved with you and what he wants to achieve by arguing with you. Having gathered these valuable insights you will be well prepared to develop a counter-strategy.

So far, so good. Where's the danger? It is just that if you are, as we shall assume, a decent, fair-minded human being you run the risk of seeing your opponent's point of view to the detriment of your own. You may even end up sympathizing with him! You're supposed to be trying to win this argument for goodness sake! If you wanted to sympathize with people you should have bought a book on counselling. Seriously, it is good to see things from the opposing point of view but you must at all costs remember where your own advantage lies and do not make the mistake of being too fair-minded.

Possum

The possum is noted for its ability to deter an aggressor by playing dead. The arguing ploy does not call for you to imitate death but merely to collapse in an undignified heap under the force of your opponent's arguments. Then, having given him the pleasure of apparently winning the argument, you proceed to ensure that the actual victory is yours.

An example will make things clearer. Steve contacted a firm of printers and asked them to produce 5,000 leaflets of A4 size. A few weeks later what actually turned up was a batch of 4,000 A5 leaflets. Steve phoned the company and gave them hell. They hadn't a leg to stand on and knew it, so they caved in, grovelled a good deal, and promised a substantial refund to put matters right. Steve retired the victor. He was a busy man and therefore it was only by chance some months later that it came to light that the promised refund had never been received. Once more he phoned the printers and received an abject apology and a promise that the refund was on its way. Again pressure of business drove the matter from Steve's mind and by the time he thought of it again a year had gone by. When he finally checked he found out that the money had never been received. Of course, part of Steve's problem was a result of his own sloppiness in keeping a check on the situation. But *Possum* depends on for its success on the fact that people are often too busy to keep tabs on everything for which they are responsible. It is therefore important to remember that apparently 'winning' the argument is only part of the battle; you have to remember to collect your winnings. An experienced Possum player may yet rob you of the real victory and end up laughing up his sleeve at you. Only concrete results count as a real victory.

Sir Humphrey

This technique is named after the Machiavellian civil servant in the old television series *Yes, Minister*. In the Civil Service itself the ploy is known as *Kick It Around Until You Lose It*. It works like this: you are presented with a proposal to which you are fundamentally opposed. To argue openly against it would be unwise since you are well aware that your superiors are committed to this course of action. What do you do? You immediately espouse the cause with every ounce of enthusiasm you can muster. If at all possible you get yourself put in charge of getting the new measures implemented. It is vital that at no stage do you let your true feelings show.

Having established a reputation as a true champion of the measures you seek to undermine, you launch a covert attack.

You may, for example, offer to set up an advisory body to discover the best way to initiate the new proposals. Naturally this body will need expert advice and you therefore arrange for the appropriate experts to prepare lengthy, time-consuming reports. Of course, more time will be consumed while everybody concerned studies the reports and gives their reactions.

In short, while giving the appearance of a staunch enthusiast held back by inevitable delays you quietly ensure that progress is made at a snail's pace. If it is suspected that someone is deliberately delaying the proposals you complain loudly at the incompetence and intransigence of your colleagues.

It goes without saying that your investigations will come up with numerous difficulties that stand in the way of these proposals being implemented. While insisting loudly that these objections are utterly futile you nevertheless will feel yourself duty bound to investigate them fully and fairly.

With luck and the passage of sufficient time you will find that circumstances change so that it will be safe to drop the whole issue.

Manipulative Arguments

Most, though not all, manipulation is practised in family arguments for the very sound reason that we are most susceptible to emotional pressure from those closest to us. The essence of all manipulation is to try to use an opponent's emotions to get him to do things that reason alone would forbid. The main weapon of the manipulator is guilt. It need not be guilt *about* anything because as human beings we all seem to carry around a ready supply of unattached guilt that can be stimulated by the right choice of words.

Parents and children are among the very worst manipulators. The parental games have titles like *What Would Your Mother Say?* or *What Have I Done to Deserve This?* I have made it clear earlier in the book that I do not consider that men and women are markedly different when they argue. Some people would be pleased to think that women are the experts at manipulation but that is quite wrong. No one with half an eye could fail to see that men do it too and are just as efficient at it.

What Would Your Mother (Father) Say? is a common technique to try to bring a wayward youngster to book. It relies on the guilt generated when one parent tells you that your actions or opinions would hurt the other parent. In these situations the other parent is always absent and frequently dead. For some reason the technique works better when the injured party is dead. A typical scenario goes something like this:

'Mum, I've given up medical school. I never wanted to be a doctor and now I've got a chance to do what I really want and go on the stage.'

'*What Would Your Father Say?* He struggled all his life to give you a decent education so that you could have a better start in life than we did. He died of a heart attack at 60 through working so hard. And now you want to be an actor?'

If this sounds like the script of a bad sitcom it is not surprising – many family arguments sound that way. There are many variants on the same theme all with similar names such as *This Will Kill Your Mother* or, for the parent who feels sufficiently confident to do his or her own suffering there is *How Can You Do This to Me?*

Children are by no means innocent when it comes to manipulation. They play games like *All The Other Kids Are Allowed To* or *Why Do You Have to Ruin My Life?* or (for grown-up children) *Why Did You Ruin My Life?* Again the technique is simply to try and load your victim with enough guilt to let you get your own way. Funnily enough in these situations there may not even be any concrete advantage to be won. In family arguments making your opponent suffer pangs of guilt may in itself be sufficient reward.

Husbands and wives play very complicated manipulative games like *Heads I Win Tails You Lose.* The rules of this game are so crazy that it is hard to explain how it works. The basis is a sort of *Reverse Psychology* into which you throw a good dose of guilt, some anger, and a hefty measure of reproach.

For example, Brian and Kate want to go out for the evening. She wants to go to the cinema; he wants to go to the pub. The baby-sitter is about to arrive and they have still not decided where to go. The essence of this game lies in the utterly insincere offers of both parties to accept their opponent's point of view.

BRIAN: OK then, let's go to the cinema. I don't care. It makes no difference to me.

KATE: What, and have you sitting there looking grumpy all evening? No thank you! If you want to be childish about it then let's go to the pub and have done with it. But you really shouldn't drink so much; you know it's not good for you.

BRIAN: You see? You don't really mean it, do you. You always were a selfish bitch. Well, I don't care, we'll go to the bloody pictures if that's how you feel!

We don't really need to go on. An argument of this sort can last for hours. I remember once spending a whole evening walking the streets of Cambridge with my wife arguing over where we should go and, eventually, going home early to a surprised baby-sitter. Yes, I confess it, I do it too! Clearly the argument develops a life of its own. This is an interesting characteristic of many arguments: they cease to be about what they are about and end up being about a whole set of things you never suspected. In this case you start with a simple disagreement that suddenly becomes a battleground in which two people fight out the routine discontents and grievances that develop in even the happiest marriage. Grudges are paid off, scores settled, pecking order confirmed or challenged. It all has nothing at all to do with where the night out is eventually spent. Often, when a happy outcome is possible, the couple finish stropping their claws on each other and then spend a happy evening doing something entirely different.

How else are people manipulated? Often public speakers, priests, politicians, rabble-rousers, lawyers and others of low character use manipulation to get the effect they want. Lawyers have a saying: 'If you can't defend your client defend the flag.' It means that when you have no real case you can always resort to a high-sounding defence of some supposedly noble principle such as Truth, Freedom, Justice or the Greater Good.

Other public speakers will play games such as *Lightning Conductor* to manipulate the public. Just think how successful Hitler was in using the Jews as his *Lightning Conductor*. He was an extreme example but don't let that lull you into a false sense of security; manipulators are at work all the time. They are easily spotted because their arguments trade on emotion rather than logic. But emotions are powerful stuff and a manipulator who has managed to work people up to a sufficient pitch may be very dangerous to oppose openly. This can happen even in an apparently 'good' cause. Remember, for example, what happened during the Falklands War? Within days of being told that 'our boys' were going to defend 'our people' from a brutal military dictatorship, British people who could not have found Argentina (let alone the Falklands) on a world map, and who had never seen an Argentinian in their lives, were talking about 'the Argies' and reading newspaper headlines saying 'Gotcha!' This, whether the purpose was good or bad (and I am offering no judgement here), was blatant manipulation of people by their leaders to win an argument by the use of emotion rather than reason. People who tried to oppose the use of force were then quickly shouted down as unpatriotic, even traitorous.

Summary

- Be persistent.
- Be sure of your facts and figures. Be specific. Name your sources.
- Practise picking holes in other people's arguments. Don't assume that a 'fact' offered by your opponent is true. Ask for details. Demand to know the source. Consider the motivation of whoever brought the fact to light.
- If you can point out an error in your opponent's argument, or can disprove your opponent's facts, do so as loudly as possible.
- Surprise your opponent with unexpected bits of information, but make sure that they are correct and up to date.
- Watch out for those forceful and dominant people who can bludgeon their way to victory by sheer force of personality. Unless you are equally forceful and dominant, they are impossible to beat. Don't play out of your league.
- Don't try to bully a bully. Keep calm in the face of aggression.
- Have the wit and presence of mind to grasp the essentials in an argument, and you may be able to score a speedy and concise victory.
- Look out for false logic in your opponent's arguments, and avoid it in your own.
- In some circumstances it is wise to refuse to be drawn into an argument. If nothing can be achieved by arguing, don't

give your would-be opponent the satisfaction of being taken seriously.

- If you want to negotiate, try splitting the argument up into its component parts to see if there are any areas where you and your opponent agree.
- Attempt to get round an opponent by appealing to him as a human being and enlisting his sympathy. But be subtle; don't let him see through you.
- Consider using a third party as a scapegoat to get your opponent on your side.
- Use distracting tactics to steer your opponent away from areas you would rather avoid. They won't help you win an argument but they may keep you from losing one.
- Learn how to avoid an open argument by skilfully getting your opponent to accept your ideas as his own.
- Try to see an argument from your opponent's point of view, but never forget where your own advantage lies.

CHAPTER THREE

Levelling the Playing Field

So far we have discussed the tactics and strategy of argument. However, being successful in arguing requires more than merely mastering a set of ploys. There are a number of wider issues that we should consider. An argument is often a very complex social interaction and all sorts of factors may affect its outcome. We must be aware of when the confrontation takes place, where it takes place, the sort of mood the contestants are in, the way in which they conduct themselves, the non-verbal signs they may use to try to influence each other, and so on. This section is dedicated to exploring these wider issues with a view to increasing your arguing power even further.

Scales

In each argument you should develop the habit of summing up for yourself the balance of advantages that you and your opponent may have. In most cases this may be simple, for example, you want a raise, the boss does not have to give you one – the advantage is with the boss. However, the balance may change and it is necessary to keep an eye on such changes and be aware when they work for or against you. The boss who did not feel inclined to give you a raise last month may change his mind when he finds that an important project, which just happens to be at a crucial stage, is in your care. If you left now he would be hard put to find a replacement soon enough. Now is the time to ask about that raise again!

Of course, you must also be on the lookout for changes that work to your disadvantage. These may happen without any great clamour but can affect you just the same. I vividly remember finishing a mammoth project that had taken four years to complete and feeling pretty pleased with myself. We were on schedule and on budget and sales were looking good. After a brief period of euphoria the truth dawned on me. Having finished the project I was without any bargaining power at all! My assistant was suddenly moved to other work (after all, what does someone with no project need with an assistant?) and I was left kicking my heels waiting for something to do. The boss, of course, was quietly enjoying reminding me of my lack of bargaining power.

Balance of advantages can be extremely complicated. In a family, for example, there will both practical and emotional considerations and it may be very hard to assess where the advantage lies. Most of the time it won't matter, but when there is a crack in the domestic harmony you will soon see everyone struggling for whatever power they think they can muster. Power may be wielded by different members of the family in different ways. One spouse may earn considerably more than the other, for example, and therefore may have financial dominance. A parent who is primarily a homemaker may have aquired authority over the day-to-day running of the home and the routines of its inhabitants. A parent or older sibling may have the advantage of physical power, by virtue of being tall and strong, even if that power is never used in physical violence. A younger sibling may gain power through being 'the baby', and may exercise it either unknowingly or through emotional manipulation.

Normally, members of a family realize that they are interdependent but, at times when things go wrong, each tries to use his or her portion of the power as a lever to gain an advantage. Your job, as a winner of arguments, is to evaluate your own position and those of your colleagues, business rivals or family members as accurately as possible. Then decide what it is you want and whether your own position is strong enough to enable you to get it.

If you do not have an instinctive feel for these things you should carry out what in management jargon is known as a SWOT analysis. The acronym stands for Strengths, Weaknesses, Opportunities, Threats. If you list all these for any given situation you should end up with a pretty good idea of just where you stand.

Having decided on what you think the balance of advantage is, you must test the water to see if your opponent is also aware of how things stand. This will require a little gentle probing. Rather than rushing headlong into an argument, try, if you can, to circle the subject warily, sensing how your adversary is likely to react. People do not always realize when the advantage is with them. Also there are people whose instinct is to attack savagely even if they are in a weak position. To return for a moment to the example of asking your boss for a raise, you may find that, even though your position is strong and his business would suffer if he lost you, he will still react aggressively because he perceives that to give in would undermine his authority as boss. I make no apology for repeating this point: never expect people to act rationally. Human beings can use reason, but they are seldom controlled by it.

Setting and Set

Timothy Leary, the high priest of the 1960s psychedelic move-
ment, used to make the point that the effects of LSD are influ-
enced enormously by the setting in which it is taken and the
state of mind of the person who is taking it. He referred to
these variables as 'setting and set'. In the context of arguments
the two are closely related. When you get into an argument
you are also entering territory where anything can happen. You
may be pleasantly surprised that you have encountered a like
mind with whom you can happily exchange ideas, or you may
meet with an attack that can range from sharp words to physical assault. Often the reaction is unpredictable. People who
argue are frequently in the grip of atavistic forces they do not
even begin to understand.

There are several ways in which we can control setting and
set. The mood of the participants in an argument will be
crucial to the outcome and you should, if possible, seek to
adjust the mood so that it works in your favour. An example
should make the point. Joe Preston turns up late for work
every morning. In every other respect he is a model employee,
bright, hardworking and full of good ideas. But by the time he
gets out of bed everyone else is ready for elevenses.

Scenario 1

Harry, Joe's department head, waits for him at the main
entrance one morning. As Joe enters Harry says loudly, 'Mr
Preston, you're late again, come and see me in my office,
please!' When Joe arrives he is given a loud and lengthy
dressing-down that can be heard all over the office.

Scenario 2

Harry waits for Joe to get to his office, take off his coat and read his post. Then he phones him and says, 'Joe, could you nip into my office for a moment?' When Joe arrives Harry starts discussing routine matters for a few minutes. He takes care to keep the atmosphere friendly and even cracks the odd joke. When he judges the time is right he says, 'Joe, we're very pleased with the work you've been doing for us but we have a bit of a problem with your time-keeping. What can we do to sort this out?'

It has to be said that both scenarios would probably have the effect of improving Joe's punctuality but the second, which warns him while not denting his self-esteem, is likely to have the more beneficial long-term effects. Scenario 1 can only initiate a heated and acrimonious argument. Joe has been backed into a corner and can either fight or find himself forced into sulky and resentful acquiescence. In Scenario 2 he has not only been told that his work is good, but he has also been given a chance to suggest an answer to the problem himself.

However, the possibilities do not end there. A ruthless manager, or one driven to the limit of his patience by having his warnings repeatedly ignored, might start with Scenario 2 and then, when his victim is suitably relaxed, bring out a *Sandbag*. For example, in one company I worked for, two of the employees were asked to keep a diary of the miscreant's movements and, when enough evidence had been accumulated, he was summoned to the MD's office. A pleasant chat ensued at the end of which the unfortunate man was presented with the diary, accused of gross misconduct, and sacked on the spot. Personally I think this is a despicable technique but it does demonstrate one of the ways in which control of mood can influence an argument.

Humour is one of the most powerful weapons available to you when trying to lighten someone's mood. You don't have to be Harry Enfield or Billy Connolly to make a few light-hearted remarks that will keep the conversation friendly. Also, without giving the impression that you are being in any way flippant, you can communicate to your opponent that the subject you are arguing about is not exactly a matter of life or death. Humour can do much to help arguers keep a sense of proportion. If you are the sort of person to whom humour does not come naturally you can always try to copy things you have heard other people say. But beware! A badly told joke is far worse than no joke at all. Anyone who remembers Mrs Thatcher trying to tell jokes (the point of which always eluded her) will know what I mean. The element of humour in an argument has the effect of saying to your adversary, 'Look, we may be disagreeing over this point but I still like you and, once this argument is out of the way, our relationship will remain undamaged.'

There are many other things you can do, both positive and negative, to affect mood. For example, instead of having your argument in the office, you can arrange to go for a drink after work and sort out your problems in the relaxed atmosphere of your local pub. Of course, this works in reverse. If you feel it is necessary you can corner someone at a time when he is feeling low, for example, at the end of the day when he is tired and looking forward to going home. You can heighten the tension by keeping him standing while you are comfortably seated. You can have other people at the meeting to back you up so that he feels threatened and outnumbered. The permutations are endless.

All the foregoing assumes that you are in control of the mood. But what if your opponent has the whip hand? There are things you can do to try to counter the negative mood he has created. You can try humour, though if he is determined to have a row it may not work. You can refuse to take him seriously and brush his remarks airily aside, though if he is your boss or in some position of authority this is a risky strategy. You can do things to interrupt the meeting and break the mood that he has created (for example, you could get a colleague to summon you to take an urgent phone call right in the middle of the argument).

There is another aspect to this whole question of mood and it concerns your ability to judge the mood of your adversary. We are all aware that our moods fluctuate from day to day, or within a single day, or even from minute to minute. Indeed some people are so volatile that it is hard to keep up with their mood swings. A small disagreement with a friend or colleague may pass almost unnoticed one day but, if it catches us at the wrong moment, it can spark a full-blown row. Therefore it is imperative that when an argument is in the offing you have as accurate a picture as possible of the mood your opponent is in. Often this is simple. Most of us telegraph our moods to any observer by our facial expressions and body language. All you need do is be sensitive enough to look closely at the other person and see what he is telling you. Tight jaw muscles, clenched fists and a glowering expression would suggest that a light-hearted approach should be tried with extreme caution. Some people, however, are adept at deliberately hiding their mood. They can appear jovial when they are angry; they can seem friendly when they are out to get you. There are even people who have their wires so tangled that they seem fierce even when they mean no harm at all. There are no easy answers to judging moods of this sort. The only real remedy is plenty of experience. After someone has bitten you once or twice you will know what his smiles are worth. But also, if you take the trouble to observe people closely, you will start to notice how false moods do not quite ring true. It is hard to pretend you are in a good mood if you are not. You may be able to smile and appear jovial but there is always something a little wooden about your performance that would warn a careful observer that you were not to be entirely trusted.

Another aspect of the setting that is closely related to the participants' mood is the temperature of the argument. Most of the time the emotional temperature will fluctuate wildly according to the whims of the participants. But suppose someone were to try consciously to control that temperature. That would work greatly to his advantage. What we need is a thermostat.

Thermostat

Most people will advise you to keep calm at all times. A cool, clear head is by the far the best way to win an argument. This is excellent advice but, like lots of other good advice, it is hard to follow in practice. One of the most obvious features of argument is the way in which people lose emotional control. However, there are things you can do to help yourself. The most efficient way to retain control is to play *Clown*. It is much easier to keep your temper with someone for whom you have scant regard. If you fear your adversary that fear will either keep you tongue-tied or, if you are pushed hard enough, get translated into anger. However, a person whom you can despise, either secretly or openly, will find it very hard to ruffle your feathers.

This is good advice as far as it goes but it leaves a lot out. First, though it is true that you should stay calm you need not always appear calm. If you are old enough to remember the more traditional forms of education you will probably recall teachers who could terrorize a whole class into submission with astounding displays of rage. The rage was, for the most part, synthetic and could be manufactured to suit the occasion. 'Losing your temper' can work very well just as long as you remember never actually to lose your temper. If you want an example just watch politicians thundering with righteous indignation about some scandal or other. Anyone who believes that they are genuinely angry is guilty of stunning naivety.

Second, you should judge carefully whether there is any advantage to be gained from making your opponent lose his temper. If you are sure of the person you are dealing with then a carefully planned campaign of provocation might be just what you need to get him off guard. But beware that your plans do not misfire and earn you a black eye. Arguments are, as we have seen, highly emotional occasions. In spite of every good resolution you may have made to the contrary there is a good chance that you will lose your temper. If this happens here are a few shreds of reason you should try to retain as the red mist descends. First, do not lash out. Argument, we decided earlier, is supposed to be a safety valve to avoid physical violence, not a prelude to it. Also you should try not to descend to the level of mere abuse. While coasting on the crest of an adrenaline high you may find satisfaction in screaming obscenities at your adversary but your loss of control will make you look foolish and vulgar in the eyes of onlookers. Worse, it will seriously devalue your arguments. Finally, never make threats that you are unwilling or unable to carry out. You will only succeed in making yourself a figure of fun.

Clockwatcher

A close relative of *Thermostat*, *Clockwatcher* deals with the timing of an argument. It is more of a preparation than a technique in its own right. You may play *Clockwatcher* in attacking or defensive mode. If you attack then you will decide on the timing of an argument to suit your own convenience. This can be done in several ways. We have probably all, at some time, tried waiting until someone is in a good mood before trying to persuade him to our point of view. That is one version of *Clockwatcher*. Another was played very successfully by a friend of mine who, when his secretary told him that an angry client was on the phone, would make an excuse for not taking the call. He would then wait and phone his opponent at home in the evening, on a Sunday morning, or at some other unexpected and inconvenient time. He was even known to turn up on someone's doorstep and carry the battle into the opponent's own home. The power of surprise was such that he usually got away with it. When the startled opponent objected that this was an unsuitable time for a business discussion, Steve would disingenuously answer that he had been so anxious to resolve these unexpected problems that he had lost no time in getting in touch.

Always try to make sure that arguments take place at a time of your choosing and are not thrust upon you at the whim of others. You should also extend this caution to all the other circumstances surrounding the occasion, particularly the location. Some people assume that you should always try to force an opponent to come to you and do battle on your territory. This may often be to your advantage, but also consider the advantage of boldly invading space where the adversary thought he was safe. Steve's trick of turning up on doorsteps may have been extreme but it was devastatingly effective.

I used to deal with a firm of book distributors whose incompetence was legendary. Unhappily for me I only found out just how bad they really were when it was too late. However, they did have one area in which they excelled. When criticized (and, God knows, they had enough experience of this), they would invite their client to a meeting to thrash out the problems. On arriving you would be presented with an agenda. And this was what was so clever. Producing an agenda looked, on the surface, like a helpful and efficient way to address problems. What it was, however, was a ruse to gain control of the argument before it even started.

So, I repeat, always make sure you retain control of all the circumstances surrounding your argument.

Psychology

We have looked at some of the ploys that are used in argument and the ways in which they can help you to win. However, arguing is about more than just choosing the right tactics. It is also about having the correct attitude and approaching your opponent in the right manner. Naturally what is 'correct' or 'right' will change from one situation to another but there are some basics that you need to be sure of.

The first thing you need is confidence in your case. We have touched on this before but it is well worth mentioning again. Unless you believe in the justice of your own cause you cannot expect to be able to convince others. Of course, there are people who make a profession of arguing and may be able to convince you that the moon is made of green cheese while not holding that view themselves. However, I assume that if you are one of those then you do not need this book.

There are also people who seem to have been born with so much confidence in their own rectitude that they cannot conceive of ever being wrong. This makes them powerful arguers but it can eventually work to their disadvantage. Unless you can take unwelcome advice and sometimes admit to the possibility that you might be wrong you run the risk of becoming dogmatic and domineering. The career of Margaret Thatcher stands as a warning to those unable to consider themselves capable of error.

Assuming that you have convinced yourself that you are in the right, how will you go about convincing others? Remaining confident is not always easy, especially if you are under pressure. Maybe, however, even if you cannot be confident there are things you could do to seem so. How do confident people behave? What signals do they give that show they feel at ease?

There are a number of body-language signs that you can use to try to create an air of confidence. First you should be aware that when people feel at ease they move at a slower, more relaxed tempo than people who are nervous. This is something you can force yourself to imitate even if it belies how you really feel. If you know that you are going into a tense situation where you may be faced with opposition then prepare by consciously breathing slowly and deeply. If possible, take a few minutes to sit quietly and calm yourself down. A simple relaxation technique will also help: go through each part of your body, alternately tensing and relaxing your muscles. You will find that tension builds up in certain areas and that the best way to disperse it is quite deliberately to tense the muscles very strongly and then let them relax. You have to devote five or ten minutes to this exercise so it is only of use where you have the time and privacy to indulge yourself. A toilet cubicle can be the ideal place. You will, of course, look ridiculous but it doesn't matter – no one can see you. Talking of toilets, it is no secret that nervousness has a distressing effect on bowels and bladder so, having completed your relaxation exercise, make sure you get full value from your visit to the loo.

What else can you do? First you must take care to avoid looking nervous. Never sit on the edge of your seat with shoulders hunched and your body bent forward in a submissive attitude. Sit back and look comfortable. Cross your legs (a clear sign that you feel at ease) but not your arms (which shows a defensive attitude). Only you can decide just how relaxed you want, or dare, to look. For example, men can put one foot up on the opposing thigh and lean well back. This is very much an 'I feel at home' gesture. On the other hand you could put your feet up on the desk in front of you and lean so far back that your chair is in danger of falling over. This, however, is a gesture that shows arrogance rather than confidence.

The next stage is to learn not to talk nervously. Nerves make you gabble. Even when you feel under no particular threat but are merely faced with an unfamiliar situation, you will automatically start to talk more quickly. If you are under attack then you may well find that you start to gabble and trip over your tongue. This is a disaster. It warns your opponent that he has you on the run and it makes it much easier for him to distract and confuse you. Learning not to do this is rather hard and takes practice. Listen to yourself and make a deliberate effort to talk slowly. Introduce pauses into your conversation that give you time to think ahead and plan what you will say. Some people cultivate mannerisms, such as taking off their spectacles and toying with them, that break the flow of conversation and allow a brief thinking space. When Harold Wilson was Prime Minister his secret weapon was his pipe. He could effortlessly disarm an aggressive questioner by pausing to light the pipe or puffing on it reflectively before giving an answer. He was able to appear perfectly calm and had an air of being completely in control of the situation (though, to show just how difficult this can be, even a past-master like Wilson was known sometimes to erupt into fits of rage under hostile questioning).

Eye contact is also important in maintaining a confident appearance. You can have too much or too little eye contact. If you fail to make proper eye contact you will look at best distracted and at worst shifty. However, in many species including our own too much eye contact is a mark of aggression and is intended to intimidate. Therefore for normal purposes you want a straightforward, friendly gaze that can be dropped or turned aside from time to time to change the rhythm of the conversation. You are trying, at least in the beginning, to create an impression of friendly interest. Of course, depending on how good an actor you are you can choose to play games. Staring at a point just in the middle of someone's forehead, for example, can have a disconcerting effect. The fact that it is nearly but not quite proper eye contact can confuse someone who is trying to make you listen to his argument. Alternatively, if you really want to provoke a row without saying something offensive you can fix your opponent with a piercing stare (remembering to keep the rest of the face immobile). This will convey an impression of cold, quietly seething anger.

How you place yourself in relation to other people is also an important factor in an argument. We all have around us an area of space that we regard as our own personal zone. How large this zone is varies between people and between cultures. Americans, who are used to bigger spaces than the British, also have a larger zone of personal space, while the Japanese are content with a much smaller area. People protect this zone and only allow strangers to enter it under special circumstances. Normally, only our most intimate acquaintances (partner, children or very close friends) are allowed inside that zone. Strangers may only enter, on sufferance, under exceptional circumstances (for example, when they stand next to each other on a crowded bus). Interestingly, when strangers are forced into each other's personal zone they will almost always ignore each other, avoiding eye contact at all costs. To enter someone's personal zone without permission is regarded as a hostile act. Naturally this permission is usually unspoken and is given by reciprocating body language.

In an argument it is common for one party to try to put the other under pressure by invading the opponent's personal zone. For example, a person making a point to his adversary may thrust his face angrily into the other's to add physical emphasis to his insulting words. Hence the recent vogue for the expression, 'Get out of my face!'. This aggressive technique can be applied with varying degrees of severity. For example, in an office, a boss who walks around his employee's desk and leans over him on the pretext of examining his work may, consciously or otherwise, be attempting to use his physical presence to apply mental pressure.

Talking of desks, it matters how you place yourself during an argument. If you sit diametrically opposite your adversary with the desk between you it will be harder to reach agreement than if you sit at two sides of a corner. If you can choose your position (and the layout of the room may make this impossible) then you should go for a 'cooperative' seating arrangement unless you are quite deliberately trying to create a confrontational atmosphere.

The gestures you use during an argument are also important. Closed gestures, such as folding your arms across your chest and tightly crossing your legs, will indicate an unwillingness to listen to your opponent. Open gestures, legs uncrossed and hands visible (especially with palms turned up) will give a more friendly and cooperative impression. It is also noticeable that people who are sympathetic towards each other show a marked tendency to mirror each other's gestures, whereas those who are in deep disagreement will use contrasting gestures.

There are a number of gestures you should avoid if you are seeking agreement. Poking and prodding the air with a forefinger is, of course, an indication of aggression and should only be used in extreme circumstances. There are other gestures that, though not openly aggressive, will not help to secure agreement. A karate chop delivered repeatedly in mid-air adds emphasis to what you say, as does bringing your fist down on a table. Both gestures are very emphatic and should not be used unless you are determined to press a point with maximum force. What is known as 'steepling' (putting the tips of your fingers together like a church steeple) looks smug and patronizing. Never use it.

Though body language is a fascinating subject it must be treated with some caution. Many of the books on the subject will suggest to you that you read someone's secret thoughts simply by looking at their gestures. This is quite untrue. Every individual is different and you need considerable experience of a person's reactions before you can come to firm conclusions about what he may be thinking. For example, the books will tell you that someone who tells lies will often give himself away by touching his mouth or face while he talks. Although this may be true of some liars it is certainly not true of many. I have come across an uncomfortably large number of people who can tell the most dreadful whoppers while appearing the very soul of sincerity. The worst liar I have ever met in my life was so plausible precisely because almost everything she said was untrue.

Transactional Analysis

The psychology of argument would be a fascinating study and would certainly fill a rather large volume all on its own. However, we are concerned with the practical purpose of winning arguments and I shall therefore consider only two aspects of psychology that will increase your understanding of what goes on in an argument. Both these ideas are taken from transactional analysis and I must again acknowledge my debt to the late Eric Berne whose writings did so much to educate the lay person in this area of psychology.

Transactional analysis (TA) is based upon the idea that each of us has within one body three separate people vying for our attention. These people are the different ego states of one person and, because each of them is 'me', we can switch effortlessly from one to the other without even noticing that a new ego state is now in charge. To start with, we each have a Child inside us. This is the child we once were and, as Freud made clear, just because a body has grown to maturity that does not mean that the Child has finished its business. In fact we retain our Child throughout life and, for many purposes, it is the most valuable part of the personality. The Child is, depending upon circumstances, the person we were at an age of between two and five years. The Child is not 'childish', which is a pejorative parental term. It is childlike – spontaneous, capable of warmth and love but also given to a single-minded quest to satisfy its own desires and quite unable to control its rage if it is thwarted. There is a form of this state, called the Adapted Child, that has learned to comply with adult directives.

The next ego state is the Parent. We learn from our own parents what the Parent should say and how it should behave. We retain this model throughout our lives. So when we wash our hands after using the toilet, for example, this is not because we have been trained in hygiene but because a Parent somewhere in us has said, for the umpteenth time, 'Now wash your hands.' The Parent's function is to remind us constantly of the moral strictures and common-sense advice that our real parents, were they present, would give to us. Those readers old enough to have lost parents will be well aware of how that voice persists in one's thoughts even long after the death of the original parent. Indeed it is such a powerful part of our mental makeup that as we get older many of us even have the rather uncomfortable sensation of actually becoming our parents and saying the same things in the same voices as were said to us many years ago.

The final ego state we must examine is the Adult. When we are in this state we offer and accept information in a matter-of-fact way. The Adult is not excitable and has no use for the emotional manipulations of the Child and Parent.

An example may help to sort out the attitudes of these three states. If you ask the Child what the weather is like today he might say, 'There's a big yellow sun in the sky.' The Parent would say, 'It may look bright but it's far too cold to play out.' The Adult would say, 'The temperature is 5 degrees Celsius, average for the time of year, and though there will be bright periods there is a 60 per cent chance of heavy showers.'

How does this help us with our study of argument? We saw right back at the beginning that when two people have different images of reality and one tries to force his image onto the other an argument is bound to occur. The same is true of ego states. If one Adult asks another a question like, 'What would you like to eat?', the answer will be, 'Steak and chips,' or something of the sort. What if the Adult were to ask the question of someone's Child? The Child is just as likely to answer, 'You never let me eat what I like!' The Adult, who deals only in facts and not moral blackmail, would merely find the reply confusing. However, the Parent would certainly know what to make of it. The Parent's reply would be, 'That's because you never eat what's good for you.' Because each of our ego states is equally the 'real me', and we can see no external indications as to which state a person may be in, arguments and misunderstandings happen easily. If, say, the Parent talks to the Child and gets an answer he feels to be inappropriate, then trouble will not be far away.

TA has much to say about personal relationships and this quick tour of the subject cannot do it justice. If you want the details read the books mentioned in the Appendix. However, there is one aspect of TA we must cover and that is what Eric Berne described as trading stamps. These are less common than they used to be, but if you think of the tokens you collect when you buy petrol and then exchange for 'free gifts' you will have the right idea.

Berne taught that people all collect an emotional equivalent of trading stamps and that they save them up until they have enough for a free gift. Emotional stamps, just like the garage ones, come in different colours and entitle us to different gifts. For example, there are Anger stamps. Each time we suffer frustration or humiliation at the hands of family, friends and colleagues we can add to our store of stamps. As soon as we have collected enough we get a free Anger. This means that we feel 'justified' in letting go of our feelings and having a good yell at someone. You could, of course, let go any time you like but, unless you have the requisite number of stamps, the Anger is not free and will carry with it a burden of guilt.

The idea of trading stamps is interesting for those of us studying arguments because it enables us to see what types of stamp those around us collect and how many it takes before they consider they have earned a free go. Observation is important. We have all come across people who, for example, need only one or two Jealousy stamps before the accusations start to fly. On the other hand there have been numerous cases reported in the Press of people who have patiently collected Frustration stamps throughout their married life before, in old age, finally getting enough for a free murder. Before you start to argue it pays to know what your opponent collects, approximately how many you think he has of any one colour, and how long it is likely to be before his free go is due. This information may be partial or, indeed, unavailable but if you have access to it you will find it a powerful tool to understanding the dynamics of any argument.

Summary

- Estimate the balance of advantages that you and your opponent have. Look out for changes that work to your advantage or disadvantage.
- Be sensitive to your opponent's mood, and seek to adjust it in a way that works in your favour.
- Stay calm. It can sometimes be to your advantage to *appear* to lose your temper, but never *really* lose your temper.
- Consider whether there is any advantage to be gained from making your opponent lose his temper. Don't incite your opponent to violence.
- Never lash out, or descend to the level of verbal abuse. It will seriously devalue your arguments.
- Never make threats that you are unwilling or unable to carry out.
- Whenever possible, choose the timing of an argument to suit your own convenience. Wait till your opponent is in a good mood, or use the element of surprise.
- Try to make sure that arguments take place at a time of your choosing and are not forced upon you by others.
- Choose a location for the argument that suits you. Sometimes it may be to your advantage to do battle on your territory, but sometimes it is better to invade your opponent's space.
- Believe in the justice of your own cause, and you will have a better chance of convincing others.
- Be confident, or if you can't *be* confident make sure that you *appear* confident.
- Practise relaxation techniques, such as deep breathing, before entering a situation that may lead to an argument.

- Don't speak too quickly. Make a deliberate effort to slow down your speech. Introduce pauses into your conversation that give you time to think ahead and plan what you will say.
- Maintain appropriate eye contact. Adopt a straightforward, friendly gaze that can be dropped or turned aside occasionally.
- Be aware of your own body language, but don't attempt to read too much from your opponent's. Adopt an open posture to give a friendly and cooperative impression. Avoid aggressive or smug gestures.

References and Further Reading

Argument is a practical subject and the best way to find out more about it is to observe good arguers in practice. Television current affairs programmes provide handsomely for anyone wishing to watch good arguers exercising their skills. In addition, the readers' letters in the serious newspapers are a rich vein for those eager to learn. The best teacher, however, is just everyday life. Observing arguments from the sidelines is the very best way of understanding how they work and what makes the difference between winners and losers. If you are interested in some of the theory behind argument here is a list of books you might find useful. There is very little in print specifically about argument but there are some books that provide a background to aspects of the subject.

Michael Billig, *Arguing and Thinking: A Rhetorical Approach to Social Psychology*, European Monographs in Social Psychology, Cambridge University Press, 1987.
An entertaining and scholarly examination of argumentation and its psychological importance in human conduct. Not a book of great practical value to the arguer but a very pleasant stroll around the social psychology of the subject. Excellent bedtime reading but not a book to turn to in an emergency.

Dean G. Pruitt and Peter J. Carnevale, *Negotiation in Social Conflict*, Open University Press, 1993
One of those distressingly heavy American academic books that seek to provide a theory for every eventuality. It comes complete with charts, graphs and statistics. Only a very dedicated student will do more than skim the text. However, a brief read will give you a few interesting ideas.

Roger Fisher, William Ury and Bruce Patton, *Getting to Yes: Negotiating an Agreement Without Giving In* (2nd edition), Business Books Limited, 1991
Well worth reading, though the idea of 'principled negotiation' seems a little naive. Maybe the Americans are right to consider the British devious. This book will certainly provide you with another perspective on argument and one that is completely at variance with almost everything you have read in this book. The work, though written by Harvard professors, is readable and entertaining. If you favour an approach that leans heavily towards agreement and away from confrontation, then this is the book for you.

Leonard Koren and Peter Goodman, *The Haggler's Handbook*, W.W. Norton & Company Inc., 1991
One of those American self-help books that seek to give you everything you ever wanted to know about a subject in a series of short, snappy paragarphs. The style is brisk and breezy. Each topic is represented by a bold heading and a paragraph of text in a box. It certainly won't strain your patience. There are some good ideas, though much of it might be seen as a bit simplistic.

Eric Berne, *Games People Play*, first published in the UK by Andre Deutsch, 1966; reprinted ...
Eric Berne is always worth reading. He is wise, witty and entertaining. This was the book that launched his reputation with the general public and it gives a brilliant insight into human interaction. Not to be missed.

Eric Berne, *What Do You Say After You Say Hello*, first published in the UK by Andre Deutsch, but long available as a Corgi paperback.
This was Berne's very best book. Though not intended for the lay person it is far more readable than many books that were. If you read no other book you must read this one.

Irving M. Copi, *Introduction to Logic*, Collier-Macmillan, 1968
Logic is always heavy going but this book, intended for students, makes it as easy as it gets. The list of fallacies given in my book was firmly based on Copi's. If you want the full story you will need stamina but it will be well worth the effort.

Index

Coping with Change at Work

Susan Jones

It was not so long ago that our place of work provided us with a stable environment when other areas in our lives were in turmoil. This no longer is the case. Changes at work, whether technological, a promotion, a new job, a redundancy, a takeover or a new management style, can be highly stressful.

This practical guide aims to enable people to make sense of their new work situation and to excel. Checklists, step-by-step guidelines and real life case studies are included, making the book invaluable for those going through a period of transition. Other issues covered include self-esteem, status, control, management issues, career progression, risk and reward.

Intended primarily for people who are going through a period of change, whether at management or staff level, this guide is also helpful for anyone who wants to learn more about this topic.

How to Think on Your Feet

Marian K. Woodall

- have you ever been caught off guard in a meeting?
- stumped by a question during a sales call?
- suffered an embarrassing silence during an interview?
- thought of the perfect response – after the conversation?

You are responsible for one half of every conversation you have…in business, in community affairs, at home…and you must be able to respond appropriately and confidently in order to succeed. This book will teach you how to think – and speak – on your feet. The author, a top lecturer and seminar leader in business communications for 24 years, shares her experience with you and shows you how to:

- answer questions impressively – even if you don't know the answer
- buy time so that you can think before you speak
- retain composure when facing difficult questions
- polish your delivery skills

Everybody needs to be able to communicate well. Using proven theory, on-target strategies, and practical examples, Marian K. Woodall will help you improve *your* end of the conversation.

Coping with Stress at Work
How to stop worrying and start succeeding

Jacqueline M. Atkinson PhD

If you:

- work better to a deadline
- leave things to the last minute, then do them in a panic
- constantly feel in a rush
- feel full of dread at the thought of going to work
- often skip lunch
- stay late at the office, or take work home
- get tired, irritable and depressed

then you are suffering from stress. And if your way of dealing with it is to have another cup of coffee or reach for a cigarette, switch on the television or pour yourself a stiff drink you are making the problems worse.

This book offers original and varied ways of combating stress in the workplace. It will help you deal sensibly and practically with stress in a way that suits you and your working environment. You will discover your own stress triggers and look at resolving and easing stressful situations; you will learn how to relax, manage your time, and deal with problems before they deal you an ulcer.

COPING WITH CHANGE AT WORK	0 7225 3130 3	£6.99	☐
HOW TO THINK ON YOUR FEET	0 7225 2963 5	£4.99	☐
COPING WITH STRESS AT WORK	0 7225 3095 1	£4.99	☐
HOW TO TALK SO PEOPLE LISTEN	0 7225 2958 9	£6.99	☐

All these books are available from your local bookseller or can be ordered direct from the publishers.

To order direct just tick the titles you want and fill in the form below:

Name: ....

Address: ....

....

....Postcode ....

Send to Thorsons Mail Order, Dept 3, HarperCollins*Publishers*, Westerhill Road, Bishopbriggs, Glasgow G64 2QT.

Please enclose a cheque or postal order or your authority to debit your Visa/Access account —

Credit card no: ....

Expiry date: ....

Signature: ....

— up to the value of the cover price plus:
UK & BFPO: Add £1.00 for the first book and 25p for each additional book ordered.
Overseas orders including Eire: Please add £2.95 service charge. Books will be sent by surface mail but quotes for airmail dispatches will be given on request.

24-HOUR TELEPHONE ORDERING SERVICE FOR ACCESS/VISA CARDHOLDERS — TEL: 0141 772 2281.